# A Corporate Solution to Global Poverty

# A Corporate Solution to Global Poverty

How Multinationals Can Help the Poor and
Invigorate Their Own Legitimacy

*George Lodge and Craig Wilson*

Princeton University Press ❧ *Princeton & Oxford*

Copyright © 2006 by Princeton University Press
Published by Princeton University Press, 41 William Street,
Princeton, New Jersey 08540
In the United Kingdom: Princeton University Press, 3 Market Place,
Woodstock, Oxfordshire OX20 1SY

All Rights Reserved

LIBRARY OF CONGRESS CATALOGING-IN-PUBLICATION DATA

Lodge, George C.
A corporate solution to global poverty : how multinationals can help
the poor and invigorate their own legitimacy / George Lodge and Craig Wilson.
p.   cm.
Includes bibliographical references and index.
ISBN-13: 978-0-691-12229-8 (cloth : alk. paper)
ISBN-10: 0-691-12229-6 (cloth : alk. paper)
1. Social responsibility of business—Developing countries. 2. International
business enterprises—Moral and ethical aspects—Developing countries.
3. Poverty—Developing countries. I. Wilson, Craig, 1968– II. Title.
HD60.5.D44L63 2006
362.5′5765—dc22        2005055238

British Library Cataloging-in-Publication Data is available

This book has been composed in Adobe Caslon

Printed on acid-free paper. ∞

pup.princeton.edu

Printed in the United States of America

1   3   5   7   9   10   8   6   4   2

*For Susan Lodge and Arlene Wilson*

# Contents

# Acknowledgments

In writing this book we received valuable assistance from many. We especially thank the development practitioners, professionals from nongovernmental organizations (NGOs), analysts from socially responsible investment funds, and business executives who provided insights from their real-world experiences.

Among representatives of NGOs, Ray Offenheiser, head of Oxfam America, and Jeremy Hobbs, head of Oxfam International, contributed insights; Juliette Bennett and Scott Greathead of World Monitors provided us with valuable data on NGOs and especially their impact on the apparel industry. We received useful feedback from Michael Kelly of the International Chamber of Commerce and drew considerably from the work of the high-minded people associated with the World Business Council for Sustainable Development.

Of those associated with governmental and intergovernmental development agencies, Sirkka Korpela and Sahba Sohbani of the Business Partnership Program of the United Nations Development Program (UNDP) were sources of informative explanations. Staff of the UN's Commission on the Private Sector and Development kept us abreast of the Commission's thinking and provided valuable comments on our proposed World Development Corporation, as did Bruce Jenks of the UNDP's Bureau for Resources and Partnerships. Holly Wise, director of the Global Development Alliance of the United States Agency for International Development (USAID), provided useful information about its activities; and we had insightful advice and comments from numerous staff and friends working in the various UN agencies, the World Bank Group, the OECD, and the IMF.

In the corporate world, Washington CySip, founder and chairman of Asia's largest accounting and consulting firm, SGV and Co., was an early supporter of the idea of a World Development Corporation; Dawn G. Rittenhouse, director of Sustainable Development for DuPont Corporation, was most helpful in describing the development activities of her company; Lord Holme, adviser to Shell's chairman, kindly gave of his time; Erin Walsh at Cisco Systems helped us to understand the "Networking Academies"; and Norbert Otten and Peter Hartmann of DaimlerChrysler described for us the company's project in northeast Brazil. Special thanks go to Kurt Hoffman, director of the Shell Foundation, for his valuable ideas and insights.

At Harvard Business School, Jacqueline Archer helped us with a number of the charts in the book; Erika McCaffrey of Baker Library was most creative and resourceful in pursuing research in the library and on the Internet and in assembling the bibliography; and George's assistant, Paula Alexander, helped manage many aspects of the manuscript with her customary efficiency. We also thank John Simon for exemplary editorial assistance.

Tim Sullivan at Princeton University Press has been a valued guide and counselor, and Karen Verde was a most skillful and meticulous copy editor. Some young men, changing the world, who offered their usual impressive and incisive input were Rohan Burdett, currently helping to set up the Iraqi justice sector; David Pearl, working on multilateral institutions at the Australian Treasury; and Peter Wilson, of Delta Pearl Ltd., working with the UK's Department for International Development on security sector reform in the developing world.

Finally, the book benefited greatly from the clarity of mind and brilliant insights of Susan Powers Lodge; and an extraordinary young woman, Anita Wilson, made all the difference.

# Abbreviations

| | |
|---|---|
| AIP | Apparel Industry Partnership |
| ATCA | Alien Tort Claims Act |
| BAT | British American Tobacco Company |
| BIAC | Business and Industry Advisory Committee (OECD) |
| BPD | Business Partners for Development |
| BRAC | Bangladesh Rural Advancement Committee |
| BSR | Business for Social Responsibility |
| CARE | Cooperative for Assistance and Relief Everywhere, Inc. |
| CDI | Commitment to Development Index |
| CEP | Council on Economic Priorities |
| CFC | chlorofluorocarbon |
| CGD | Center for Global Development |
| CIPE | Center for International Private Enterprise |
| CSO | civil society organization |
| CSR | corporate social responsibility |
| DAI | Development Alternatives Inc. |
| DARPA | Defense Advanced Research Projects Agency |
| DFID | Department for International Development (UK) |
| EIR | Extractive Industry Review |
| EU | European Union |
| FDI | foreign direct investment |
| FIAS | Foreign Investment Advisory Service (World Bank) |
| GDA | Global Development Alliance (USAID) |
| GDP | gross domestic product |
| GRI | Global Reporting Initiative |
| GSB | Growing Sustainable Business for Poverty Reduction (UNDP) |
| GSDF | Global Sustainable Development Facility |
| IBC | International Business Council |
| IBLF | International Business Leaders Forum |
| IBRD | International Bank for Reconstruction and Development (World Bank) |

| | |
|---|---|
| ICC | International Chamber of Commerce |
| IFC | International Finance Corporation |
| ILO | International Labor Organization |
| IMF | International Monetary Fund |
| IPA | investment promotion agency |
| ISO | International Organization for Standardization |
| MAI | Multilateral Agreement on Investment |
| MDG | Millennium Development Goals |
| MNC | multinational corporation |
| NGO | nongovernmental organization |
| OECD | Organization for Economic Cooperation and Development |
| PETA | People for the Ethical Treatment of Animals |
| PRSP | Poverty Reduction Strategy Paper |
| RAN | Rainforest Action Network |
| SGBI | Strengthening Grassroots Business Organizations Initiative (IFC) |
| SME | small and medium-sized enterprises |
| UN | United Nations |
| UNCTAD | United Nations Conference on Trade and Development |
| UNDP | United Nations Development Programme |
| UNEP | United Nations Environment Programme |
| UNIDO | United Nations Industrial Development Organization |
| USAID | United States Agency for International Development |
| USSR | Union of Soviet Socialist Republics |
| WAIPA | World Association of Investment Promotion Agencies |
| WBCSD | World Business Council for Sustainable Development |
| WDC | World Development Corporation |
| WEF | World Economic Forum |
| WRI | World Resources Institute |
| WSSD | World Summit for Sustainable Development |
| WTO | World Trade Organization |

# A Corporate Solution to Global Poverty

# Prologue

We have written this book to help the managers of the world's multinational corporations understand and better deal with the threats to their legitimacy. After tracing the origins of the legitimacy problems plaguing global business, we argue that one key way that multinational corporations can invigorate their legitimacy is by making better use of their extraordinary resources and abilities to effect greater reduction of poverty in the world's developing countries. But they will not and cannot do this on their own; they must have the collaboration of governmental and nongovernmental development organizations.

Since the word "legitimacy" is central to our thesis, we shall state what we mean by it at the outset. A corporation's legitimacy depends upon obeying the law, but it also requires a genuine respect for and comprehension of public opinion and an understanding of the expectations of society concerning corporate behavior. And those expectations, especially in a global or multinational setting, may differ widely from the requirements of law in different operational jurisdictions. Indeed, adhering to the letter of the law while violating the "community's" principles is a recipe for long-term disaster. Today, for example, an increasing number of voices who claim to speak for the public are pressing corporations to go well beyond the requirements of the law and to contribute more effectively to the solution of such problems as environmental degradation, epidemic diseases, child labor, illiteracy and, more recently, developing-country poverty. Our focus in this book is upon the last item listed here—developing-country poverty—the one often considered to be the root of the other issues listed.

The fact is that the traditional ideas from which corporations derive their legitimacy have eroded. For example, the notion of untrammeled property rights, with the uses of property being determined by competition to satisfy consumer desires in an open marketplace, has given way to the realization that property rights are highly constrained and that, quite apart from consumer desires, there are broader community needs that the corporation must serve.

From another perspective, one senior business executive we spoke to referred to "responsibility fatigue" when he reviewed the previously extraneous, but now common, set of global problems that are routinely discussed in the world's most important boardrooms. All of the business executives to whom we spoke said much the same thing: running a successful business is hard enough—out-competing rivals, remaining innovative, dealing with risk, keeping down costs and achieving profits, adhering to a wide variety of national and international laws. But at the same time these executives realized that much is now expected of them beyond achieving profits—community expectations are increasing, and changing, and hard to pin down—and yet they need to meet these expectations.

Often, however, the corporate response to these expectations is hamstrung by a lack of legitimacy, a crippling but hitherto inadequately diagnosed problem that reduces the ability of big business to respond as meaningfully as it otherwise could. This is something of a classic catch-22. Managers of global corporations—everyone from the CEOs to their subordinates far down the corporate ladder—who lack the necessary legitimacy can't effectively respond to these challenges because their response requires them to cooperate with people (the community) who don't trust their intentions. The community, broadly speaking, is no longer satisfied that managers and their corporations are fully law-abiding as they go about increasing shareholder value. Communities want more. But they don't trust managers to provide "more" because they haven't in the past. And so the cycle of distrust continues. Demands and expectations are rising in the face of declining legitimacy.

In this book, we aim to help corporate managers find a way to regain their legitimacy, which will allow them to respond to the demands increasingly being made on their organizations to do more to alleviate the poverty that plagues much of the world. But they can do so only with the help of leaders of international development institutions and nongovernmental organizations concerned with poverty reduction. Together, these two groups—corporations and development organizations—can make more effective use of their resources and capacities to ameliorate developing-country poverty.

We realize that we are not alone in recognizing the decline of corporate legitimacy around the world. Let us list a few points. First, this decline is rooted in a number of factors, including revelations of large-scale abuse in corporate governance as well as changing public expectations concerning the impact of global companies on society. In addition, the old ideas from which multinational corporations (MNCs) derive their legitimacy are proving inadequate: maximizing shareholder value by competing to satisfy consumer desires in the marketplace is not enough. Corporations are increasingly being pressed to serve a variety of community needs. Normally this pressure is applied by governments that define those needs and impose regulations to ensure that they are met. The problem is that there are some needs—notably poverty reduction in the developing world—which many governments are not only unwilling or unable to fulfill by themselves but are also reluctant or unable to press corporations to address. Thus, the corporation suffers a legitimacy problem in that it is not fulfilling expectations; it is not serving community needs—including poverty reduction—as well as it can and as well as many think it should.

Second, we found these legitimacy problems to be broad-based and unrelenting. There are no signs on the horizon of the decline in MNC legitimacy abating or reversing. This is a huge concern for global business. Presenting a plan on how MNCs can navigate the gap is imperative to prevent their floundering through the process, which would cost us—all of us—precious time and resources.

Third, our research showed that in recent times the world's largest companies have often responded imaginatively, if sometimes awkwardly and haphazardly, to the challenge to their legitimacy, principally by working to lessen their environmental impact and better align their activities with social considerations. Notwithstanding varying views on the matter, the manifold forms of corporate social responsibility are one manifestation of this.

Fourth, it became clear that despite both this corporate response and the continuing legitimacy problem, the international consensus on the need for global poverty reduction is only growing stronger. It's as if all of the half-measures that MNCs have adopted have only spurred on those who demand more of them. And MNCs are being called on to do yet more to meet that need. This call is taking on ever greater urgency because of the continuing disappointing results of the broad array of antipoverty efforts led by national and international development organizations.

When we reviewed the work and policies of the relevant international development institutions, nongovernmental organizations (NGOs), and national governments, we discovered that the interface between their efforts and the mainstream operations of the world's major corporations was extremely limited, notwithstanding the existence of a few embryonic pilot and partnership projects. If one agrees that the world's large corporations are in fact the greatest drivers of wealth creation, then the degree of their separation from formalized international poverty-reduction efforts is startling. This lack of interaction is all the more surprising given the growing call from many quarters for MNCs to do more to help reduce global poverty and the growing reliance on public-private initiatives in other arenas. This is especially so given the fact that over the years multinational corporate investment and activity has been a—if not *the*—major factor in reducing poverty in developing countries.

Finally, we found that the international public and institutional call for multinational corporations to do more has not been accompanied by any guiding coordination or instruction. There is growing consensus on the destination, but no agreement on the way(s) to get there. Thus, business executives as well as development practitioners are often uncertain as to how to proceed. We hope this book will help the existing principal drivers of the global economy, and the leading architects of global poverty reduction—large corporations and development institutions, respectively—to coordinate their efforts for the benefit of the poor.

## The Book's Organization

The book is divided into three parts. In part 1, the first two chapters set forth the problems we address. Chief among them are global poverty and global wealth inequality, for which MNCs, rightly or wrongly, get much of the blame. They are criticized both for what they do and for what they don't do. At the same time, as we noted, the traditional ideas from which corporations derive their legitimacy have eroded. Consequently, in this first part of the book we deal with the transition that is occurring in the ideology from which corporations derive their authority. Chapter 1 speaks generally to the issue of globalization and the challenges to the legitimacy of international companies. Chapter 2 argues that the corporation's legitimacy problems can be best understood by examining the gap between the ideas upon which they rely for authority and the reality, partly of their own making, that exists around them.

Part 2 describes the key organizations that address these problems and the relationships among the organizations. We examine a sampling of MNCs, a number of NGOs, and a host of governmental and intergovernmental organizations such as the United Nations and the World Bank. We reveal a gap in the coverage of these organizations that limits their collective effectiveness in reducing poverty. In chapter 3 we go on to describe the swarm of NGOs that exploit this gap. They want MNCs to serve their purposes and to do more to reduce global poverty but they do not trust them to do it. Chapter 4 addresses the corporate response to all of this. Chapters 5 and 6 describe the international consensus and institutional structure dealing with the issue of global poverty. We note that, although many development institutions realize MNCs are the key to poverty reduction in poor countries, their willingness to act on this realization is limited by the fear of being "tainted" by business.

In the final part of the book, part 3, chapters 7 and 8 are concerned with the future: how the wealth gap can be closed; what businesses' options are; how the power of the world's global corporations can be turned toward the goal of reduction of global poverty (without in any way curtailing shareholder value); and how corporate legitimacy can be enhanced. We end by proposing a new organization to help business and development agencies achieve their poverty reduction ambitions—a World Development Corporation.

# PART I

## The Legitimacy Gap

# 1

# Introduction

Daily, in countless ways, we are reminded of the growing interdependence of the world's six billion people—processes that have collectively become referred to as "globalization." Globalization is in large part driven by the world's multinational corporations, two-thirds of which in 2005 were based in Western Europe and the United States, with the majority of the remainder headquartered in the Asia-Pacific region and Latin America. In possession of a dazzling array of new technologies, these MNCs have increased and accelerated the flows of trade, investment, and information across national borders, making themselves, for better or for worse, indispensable to human progress. Those whom they benefit have greater access to power, profits, and self-determination.

Because MNCs are at the heart of the processes that compose globalization, they have created an easy target for those who have watched globalization destroy cherished ways and erode the ability of states to control their territories. Enriching many, globalization has left many others behind, and its sometimes adverse effects on the world's life-sustaining environment cause widespread alarm. Of paramount concern to many is the failure of globalization to reduce poverty and lessen wealth inequality in developing countries. Indeed, many charge that globalization and the global corporations that drive it have made international poverty worse. Belligerence is escalating. For example, at a recent meeting of the World Economic Forum in Davos, Switzerland, antiglobalization protesters held up a sign that read, "Our resistance is as global as your oppression."[1] And in the Islamic world, globalization and the wealth it creates carry the taint of blasphemy, materialism smothering spirituality. It is significant that it is not only the followers of Al Qaeda who resent the media giants that infect the young with what the West calls "culture."

Nevertheless, even though it is and will remain deeply controversial and its progress may falter, globalization will continue. And MNCs will remain easy primary targets for those who focus on its negative consequences. This group comprises a growing band of NGOs, community groups, and even government leaders. Although the utility of MNCs is clear—they produce goods and services upon which we rely every day—their legitimacy is eroding in the face of such criticism. The more thoughtful and farsighted of their leaders are responding to the threat posed by this decline in legitimacy by searching for ways to meet expanded community expectations, provide environmental leadership, reduce global poverty, and make the world a better place, while still satisfying their shareholders. A successful strategy along these lines, especially one that works to reduce global poverty, will be the new source of MNCs' legitimacy.

Up to this point, as far as poverty reduction is concerned, the collective response of MNCs has been sporadic and frail, rich with rhetoric but poorly organized and inadequate. Furthermore, and despite obvious complementarities, their efforts have been inadequately supported by international institutions and national governments. The question, then, is how to coordinate the actions of the many interested parties and achieve the sought-after objectives.

## The Controversy

More than seventy years ago French paleontologist and theologian Pierre Teilhard de Chardin wrote, "Nothing, absolutely nothing—we may as well make up our minds to it—can arrest the progress of social Man towards ever greater interdependence and cohesion. . . . It would be easier, at the stage of development that we have reached, to prevent the earth from revolving than to prevent mankind from becoming totalized."

Teilhard spoke of "the thinking layer of the earth," "a thinking envelope," "a collective global energy." He called it "the Noosphere" (from the Greek *noos* meaning *mind*) and attributed this "phenomenon of growing consciousness on earth . . . to the increasingly advanced organization of more and more complicated elements."[2]

Teilhard was an optimist: he saw virtue in convergence. Vaclev Havel, on the other hand, in his 1995 commencement speech at Harvard University, saw conflict. He spoke of globalization as a "thin veneer" forcing interdependence even as it exacerbated tensions in the world's "underside," among cultures, religions, tribes, traditions, and nations. "Every valley cries out for its own independence or will even fight for it."

What has changed about globalization of late, especially over the last several decades, is its scale, extent, and intensity. (See box 1.1 for a definition and data and figures 1.1 to 1.5.) What makes globalization so controversial—easy to characterize in either the positive or the negative with equal ease and passion—is the uncertainty about the rules by which it is governed. So many questions are raised: Who is deciding its purposes and priorities? How are the decisions made? Who will benefit? At what cost?

While there are no easy, one-sided answers to these questions, there is considerable evidence that those who manage the world's giant corporations lie at the heart of the issue. Government policies do, of course, shape globalization, at least in countries with strong, capable governments, but even there corporate managers have found ingenious ways to use the power of their respective governments for their own corporate ends.[3] In the developing world, governments are not only fragile and often corrupt, but also invariably so eager for the benefits of corporate investment that they are not overly fussy about attendant negative consequences. Multinational corporations create jobs, bring access to credit and markets, introduce new technologies, often reduce the prices of goods and services, and increase the wealth of the host economy through payments of taxes and wage income. MNCs also, on average, pay higher wages than domestic companies. Perhaps this explains why, in 2002, 70 national governments adopted a record 248 investment-friendly legal and regulatory changes in order to attract them.[4] For example, in the 1980s Malaysia attracted several multinational semiconductor manufacturers by promising no taxation on earnings for five to ten years and guaranteeing that electronics workers would be prevented from forming an independent union.[5]

In light of the criticism of their activities, it is easy to lose sight of the undeniable benefits investment by MNCs brings to developing countries. A recent report by the McKinsey Global Institute found that

Box 1.1

### Globalization: Definition and Data

A recent review of the copious literature on globalization defines it as "the gradual integration of economies and societies driven by new technologies, new economic relationships, and the national and international policies of a wide range of actors, including governments, international organizations, business, labor and civil society (NGOs)." Here are some measures of the recent phase of globalization and its effects.

*Trade and Economic Growth*

World trade, measured by world exports of goods and services, between 1985 and 2002 tripled from $2.3 trillion to $7.8 trillion. During the same period, world nominal gross domestic product (GDP) increased by two and a half from $12.8 trillion to $32 trillion. The ratio of exports to GDP, however, fell in about a third of the 174 countries surveyed. In low-income countries the ratio fell more than 20 percent. During the seventeen-year period the share of world trade of these countries (excluding China and India) actually decreased from 3.6 percent in 1985 to 2.7 percent in 2002, implying a marginalization of poor countries. These countries' share of world GDP decreased even more drastically from 4.5 percent to 2 percent.

*International Capital*

Global inflows of foreign direct investment (FDI) increased more than ten times between 1985 and 2002 (from $58 billion to $633 billion). But the share of FDI going to low-income countries fell from an already marginal 3.3 percent to 1.1 percent. Their share of world portfolio investment (short-term capital flows into equity and bonds) decreased from 0.04 to less than 0.01 percent.

*(continued)*

*(continued)*

Thus it seems quite clear that globalization has exacerbated the inequalities among the world's countries. The rich, and China and India, have become richer, while the poor countries where 30 percent of the world's population live have drifted to the margins of the world economy, their employment and labor standards declining.

Source: Bernhard G. Gunter and Rolph van der Hoeven, "The Social Dimension of Globalization: A Review of the Literature," *International Labour Review* 143 (Geneva: International Labour Organization, 2004), pp. 7–19.

the overall economic impact of such investment has been "overwhelmingly positive despite the persistence of policies that lead to negative, unintended consequences."[6] Besides improving developing countries' standards of living, the report identified other benefits including lower prices, higher quality and broader selection of goods, and increased productivity and output among suppliers. Concluded the report: "Compared to its potential . . . it's just a drop in the bucket."

Their vulnerability to attack is in many ways a function of MNCs' efficiency. In his recent study, Brian Roach of Tufts University wrote, "What especially differentiates the modern MNC from earlier large firms is its great mobility to seek low-cost inputs to production. This transnational mobility implies that firms may be able to set nations against one another in an effort to obtain a favorable regulatory environment. Even further, recent international trade agreements may enable corporations to circumvent national sovereignty entirely."[7]

MNCs can shop the world seeking the lowest cost suppliers. Nike, the world's largest apparel retailer, contracts with foreign suppliers mostly in China, Indonesia, and Vietnam. Not a single Nike employee makes shoes. Thus, the company can move with remarkable speed to take advantage of lower costs and friendly regulation.[8] This mobility of capital, which is commonly found in the garment and apparel industries, can cause some economic dislocations in host economies but does

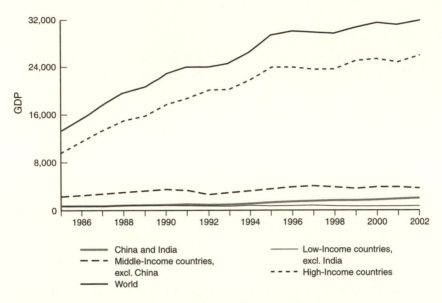

Figure 1.1. Evolution of GDP (billions of current US$). Source: Gunter and van der Hoeven, "The Social Dimension of Globalization," 2004.

not otherwise detract from the strong case for the benefits of foreign direct investment flowing into developing countries.[9] Similarly, Coca-Cola, which sells an enormous volume of products in Bangladesh, employs fewer than ten people there directly, as subcontracted firms handle most of its production and distribution.

In addition to the greater mobility of capital these days, the sheer size and reach of MNCs, which are extremely large and enormously powerful, appear to their critics to be beyond the effective control of political authority. Comparing corporate revenues with national gross domestic products, one study found that fifty-one of the world's one hundred largest economies are companies.[10] Using value-added as a measure (defined as the sum of salaries, pretax profits, and depreciation and amortization), twenty-nine of the world's largest economies are companies. In 2000, ExxonMobil, the world's largest corporation, was bigger than 180 of the world's 220 national economies and certainly much larger in economic size than most of the countries in which it operated.[11] The world's largest private corporate employer is Wal-Mart, with 1.3 million workers.[12] And these corporate giants are growing:

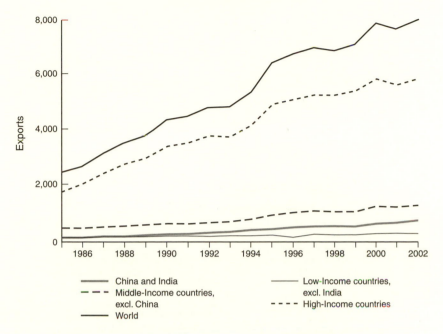

Figure 1.2. Evolution of exports (billions of current US$). Source: Gunter and van der Hoeven, "The Social Dimension of Globalization," 2004.

between 1983 and 2001, "the value of capital assets owned by the world's fifty largest corporations increased by an astonishing 696 percent."[13] Further, by the early 1990s MNCs accounted for more than two-thirds of global trade in goods and services.[14]

With all this economic power, say their critics, MNCs have achieved political power as well and so, to use the phrase Raymond Vernon applied in the United States some years ago, they are like "rogue elephants in the forest."[15] They pollute. They exploit low-cost labor. They bribe officials. They find themselves in cahoots with unsavory governments. They subvert traditional cultures. And, especially in the poor world, the states in which they operate will not or cannot control their behavior. "Corporations have invested billions to shape public and political opinion," the critics charge. "When they own everything, who will stand up for the public good?"[16]

Furthermore, despite their growth and success (there are more than 63,000 MNCs, nine times the number 30 years ago), they have failed

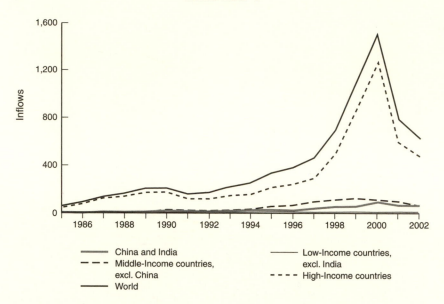

Figure 1.3. Evolution of inflows of FDI (billions of current US$). Source: Gunter and van der Hoeven, "The Social Dimension of Globalization," 2004.

to bring prosperity to much of the world.[17] Indeed, in the last twenty years, with the notable exceptions of China and India, poverty in developing countries as well as the gap between rich and poor has worsened.[18] (Issues related to poverty and wealth inequality are covered more fully in chapter 6.)

Yet, many defensibly argue that the problem with globalization is that it isn't global enough. Corporate foreign direct investment in the developing world has been concentrated in just a few countries, especially in China in recent years, with the least developed countries, where poverty is normally greatest and the process of investing most risky, receiving little. In fact, the World Bank reports that some two billion people live in countries that are becoming less globalized, among them Pakistan, Indonesia, and much of Africa and Latin America. In those regions, trade has diminished in relation to national income, economic growth has stagnated, and poverty has risen. Most Africans were better off forty years ago. The average per capita income of Muslims—from Morocco to Bangladesh and beyond to Indonesia and the Philippines—is one-half the world average. Other countries such as Botswana and Thailand have in a relatively short time been able to double average per

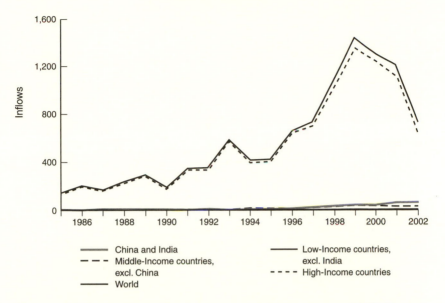

Figure 1.4. Inflows of portfolio investment (billions of current US$). Source: Gunter and van der Hoeven, "The Social Dimension of Globalization," 2004. As we explained in box 1.1, inflows to low-income countries were so low that they scarcely register on this chart.

capita income, mostly by accepting foreign investment and adopting new technologies. However, it is clear that the difference in the degree of openness around the world remains significant and is largely responsible for corresponding gaps in development, individual wealth, and the reduction of poverty. Those countries with the weakest links to the outside world are the poorest. As figure 1.6 shows, the countries that opened their economies and pursued the greatest economic openness since 1980 have vastly exceeded the economic growth rates of even the world's richest countries.

Despite the roughly $1 trillion that has been spent on grants and loans to fight poverty around the globe since the end of World War II, the World Bank reports that nearly half the world's population still lives on less than $2 a day, and one-sixth get by on less than $1 a day.[19] To quote Joseph Stiglitz, one-time chief economist of the World Bank: "Despite repeated promises of poverty reduction made over the last decade of the twentieth century, the . . . number of people in poverty has actually increased by an average of 2.5 percent annually."[20] During this

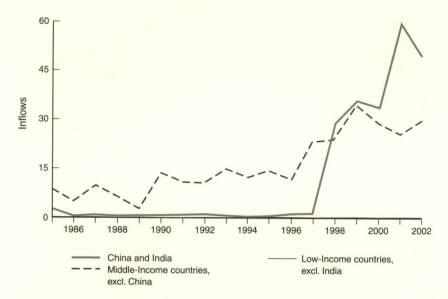

Figure 1.5. Inflows of portfolio investment in low- and middle-income countries (billions of current US$), 1985–2002. Source: Gunter and van der Hoeven. Inflows to low-income countries were so low that they scarcely register on this chart.

same period, however, many of the world's people have become much richer because of the activities of global corporations, but the inequality gap in the world has grown. "The central challenge we face today," according to UN Secretary General Kofi Annan, "is to ensure that globalization becomes a positive force for all the world's people, instead of leaving billions of them behind in squalor."[21]

The resources of the world's MNCs are central to solving this challenge. As Peter Woicke, former executive vice president of the International Finance Corporation, commented:

> Our world faces huge challenges. About 20 percent of the global population owns 80 percent of the assets, 1.2 billion people live in deep poverty, and most of the population growth in the next 20 to 30 years—an additional two billion people—will take place in the poor countries. These are challenges that go beyond the capacity of the public sector. To help address these challenges, the private sector has to take some responsibility for economic and social development as well, leading to a better world where it will be able to develop and thrive.

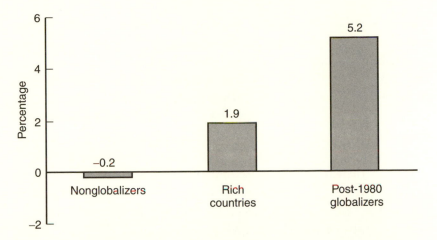

Figure 1.6. Convergence and divergence in the 1990s: Per capita GDP growth rates. Source: International Finance Corporation, May 2004 (Rapid Response Unit).

Woicke continued:

> The private sector is at the heart of the changes that need to be made to ensure a better future for developing countries. In the years to come private companies will generate most if not all of the growth; they will demand most of the resources; they will gain more responsibility for development; and they will enjoy most of the opportunities. That is the new reality.[22]

This "new reality," which includes MNCs (both in their role as targets for opponents of globalization and also in their role as part of the solution), also includes space for the swarm of vigilantes (6,000 at the last count) that has arisen to curb what they regard as corporate abuse and create new rules for the governance of globalization. These organizations are a subspecies of what are generally referred to as nongovernmental organizations or NGOs. They have enlisted the support of many governments—indeed, some 40 percent of their funding comes from governments—and have gained much influence in international organizations such as the United Nations, the World Bank, and even the International Monetary Fund.[23] Their record of achievement is impressive, ranging from producing an international treaty banning land mines "over the opposition of the most powerful bureaucracy in the world's most powerful state: the U.S. Pentagon,"[24] to pressuring giant pharmaceutical companies such as Merck and Bristol-Myers into cutting the price of HIV/AIDS drugs in poor countries. Recently the NGO, Forest Ethics, pressed Kinkos, the large American copying and printing chain, to commit to buying paper from sustainable sources, while the Rainforest Action Network extracted promises from the U.S. lumber company Boise Cascade to stop logging endangered forests.[25]

If there is such a thing as "the international community"—and we believe there is, even though it's hard to define—it seems that this community has accepted, even welcomed, the NGOs: Amnesty International, Friends of the Earth, Oxfam International, the Sierra Club, Human Rights Watch, and the rest. They are doing what no other organizations or institutions seem to be capable of doing—forcing the world to observe certain minimum standards of humanity and behavior. Although their own legitimacy is questionable in that they are essentially self-appointed, the utility of NGOs is accepted, even, in many cases, by the very corporations they attack. At their best, they reflect a global consciousness akin to that foreseen by Teilhard, rooted in moral convictions about rights and duties that transcend cultures and boundaries, which, shared by human beings everywhere, also lie at the heart of the United Nations and its many agencies.

The NGOs' emphasis on global rights and duties provides them abundant ammunition with which to attack multinationals. But given the importance of global corporations to the economy—and the polity—of the world, and their preeminent effectiveness at creating and storing wealth, developing technology, and managing resources, the continuing challenge posed to their legitimacy demands further consideration. In the next chapter we shall inspect the traditional assumptions from which managers derive their authority, their right to manage. We shall argue that the old assumptions are becoming less valid, less acceptable, and less consistent with what the managers themselves are actually doing. A "legitimacy gap" is emerging.

# 2

# The Legitimacy of Business

Before pursuing how multinational corporations and their managers can solve the legitimacy gap, it's worth considering the sources of their legitimacy over time.[1] To say that their legitimacy is now eroding is to say that circumstances and context have changed and that MNCs and their representatives must catch up.

Business derives its legitimacy from an ideology, a collection of ideas that a community uses to make values explicit and give them vitality in institutions.[2] It links values on the one hand and the real world or relevant context on the other. The main point to take to heart is that any authority experiences a "legitimacy gap" when its stated aims and purposes are at odds with those of the larger community. To take one example, in the United States of the early nineteenth century, slavery was justified in the eyes of many because slaves were deemed to be property and property rights were, according to the prevailing ideology, sacred. Furthermore, in the context of plantation agriculture, slavery was seen by some states as consistent with community need, a view justified by the notion of states' rights and a limited role for the federal government. In abolishing slavery, the Civil War changed two components of American ideology: one concerned property and the other, the power and role of the federal government. A new way of defining justice was ushered in.

Or consider the birth of the modern environmental movement. "Economy" is a value in that every community wants more benefits than costs, but what counts as a benefit and what counts as a cost changes in response to events and insights in the real world. Seabirds die with oil on their feathers, Rachel Carson writes *Silent Spring*, and the environmental movement is born. In the early 1970s, Allied Chemical, a Virginia-based manufacturer of the insecticide Kepone, found that the idea of competition in the marketplace was no longer a reliable way to define what is a cost and what is a benefit. Kepone had killed the fish in the James River and contaminated mothers' breast milk as far away as Georgia. Government was required to set standards and regulate behavior, an ideological shock to those who, along with John Locke, believed that the best government is that which governs least.

Ideology is thus a dynamic structure, a bridge that connects values to the surrounding reality in various communities at different times. It is not dogma, although many would like to make it so. It is the hymns a community sings to justify and make legitimate what it is doing or, perhaps, what it would like to do. It changes as the reality changes, but the change is invariably slow because an old ideology becomes rooted in the culture. Ideologies are changed by crises in the real world—wars, depressions, economic competition, disasters, and the like. In response to crises, institutions such as government and business change their methods of coping and in so doing depart from the old ideology (e.g., modern China's reaction to the success of a shift to free-market economics). The problem is that even as the institutions change pragmatically to adapt and compete, the old ideology (the cherished hymns) remains in place. The creation of a new ideology to justify what is happening is delayed, rendering the institutional change temporarily illegitimate. The community no longer practices what it preaches, but it hasn't learned to preach what it practices. There is thus a "legitimacy gap" between practice on the one hand and ideology on the other.

Here we come to the problem at hand, the purpose of a corporation. In Anglo-American ideology, corporations and their managers attend to the satisfaction of shareholders because shareholders own the capital and are thus endowed with the rights of property. Difficulties arise because, as Berle and Means pointed out more than seventy years ago, shareholders in the West do not really own—by any reasonable definition of ownership—most publicly held corporations.[3] They don't, they can't, and they don't want to. They are investors pure and simple, and if they do not get a satisfactory return, they move on.

So if the corporation has no owners it is not really property and thus sits in ideological limbo, controlled by a self-perpetuating hierarchy that, as we have seen recently at Enron and Tyco in the United States, for example, is apt to misbehave. Although more stringent government regulation seems rational, it is ideologically repellant to many. So, while the relevant context has changed and the institution—the publicly held corporation—adapted with speed and efficiency, the old ideology remains. The result? The corporate governance issues the world faces today.

This analysis may seem irrelevant. But ideological analysis is important to managers because it helps them to inspect their assumptions about their role, authority, and power; and to answer such questions as: By what right do I govern? What is the source of my authority and how might it be changing? For a time managers might act consistently with a prevailing ideology, but when circumstances change managers naturally respond to take advantage of, or merely to cope with, the change. In so doing they depart from the old ideology and thus are open to the charge of illegitimacy from both ends—from those who adhere to the old ideology and those who embrace the new reality. Or managers might be so imbued with the old ideology that they fail to adapt to the changes in the real world and thus become progressively inefficient and ineffective at addressing real problems.

There are a number of permutations and combinations along these lines. One example comes from the owner/manager of a paper company on the Nashua River in Massachusetts during the early days of the environmental movement. His and seventeen other companies were dumping their effluent into the river. In 1968, he "got religion" and decided he would clean up his waste. As a consequence, he went broke. And the seventeen others were still contaminating the river. When asked what he had learned from this experience, he said,

"I did what was socially responsible and paid the price."

When it was noted that the river was no cleaner, he replied, "Oh, well, that's the seventeen fellows upstream. They will learn from my example."

It was further put to him that he should consider going to the state, maybe to the government in Washington, D.C., to seek strict standards, carefully enforced, so that when he went clean everybody else would also. He replied, "Oh, no, I couldn't do that. This is the free enterprise system. Business can do the job. Keep the government out of it."

In other words, he was prepared to accept the free-rider cost, rather than see the government get involved to level the playing field.

This example relates directly to the legitimacy of MNCs and their managers. Surveys show that world opinion, including the opinion of many corporate leaders, expects multinational corporations to do more to reduce global poverty.[4] This is becoming a measure of corporate legitimacy. Those companies that find a way to reduce poverty more effectively will have more legitimacy than those who remain tied to the old ideology. And their managers will find it helpful to think about their poverty-reducing activities using a different ideological framework, because in departing from the old ideas they need new ones to ensure that their actions are perceived as just.

The current shift in ideologies can be seen as mixtures and variations of two ideal types. In 1974, one of the authors took the first component of each ideology to name them "individualism" and "communitarianism,"[5] the latter term having since been taken up by others.

First, we cover individualism. The United States provides an excellent venue in which to examine how ideology has shifted and is still shifting. Despite its claims to be pragmatic, the United States is a profoundly ideological community and, given the power and stretch of its multinational corporations, not to mention its government, the country has considerable global impact.

The traditional ideology of the United States exemplifies individualism. It first came to America in the eighteenth century, having been set down in seventeenth-century England by John Locke, among others. These ideas found fertile soil in the vast, underpopulated wilderness of America. Although individualism has been buffeted, eroded, and in many ways replaced by communitarian practices, particularly in times of crisis, its ideas continue as a kind of religion. As Samuel Huntington opined, these values "are at the very core of [our] national identity. . . . Americans cannot abandon them without ceasing to be Americans in the most meaningful sense of the word—without in short becoming un-American."[6]

Because they are so familiar, we can state the five interconnected components of American individualism briefly.

1. *Individualism.* This is the atomistic notion that the community is no more than the sum of the individuals in it. Fulfillment lies in an essentially lonely struggle in what amounts to a wilderness in which the

fit survive and those who don't survive are somehow unfit. Closely tied to individualism is the idea of *equality*, in the sense implied by the phrase "equality of opportunity," and the idea of *contract*, the inviolate device by which individuals are tied together as buyers and sellers, employers and employees. In the U.S. political order, individualism evolved into *interest-group pluralism*, which has become the preferred means of directing society.

2. *Property rights*. Traditionally, the best guarantee of individual rights lay in the sanctity of property rights. By virtue of this concept, the individual—and the corporation as well—were assured freedom from the predatory powers of the sovereign; and from this notion the corporate manager derived the authority to manage. From it also came the idea that the purpose of the corporation was to satisfy the owners, that is, the shareholders.[7]

3. *Marketplace competition*. Adam Smith most eloquently articulated the idea that the uses of property are best controlled by each individual proprietor, motivated by his or her self-interest, competing in an open market to satisfy consumer desires. This has been made explicit in U.S. antitrust law and practice.

4. *Limited state*. In reaction to the powerful hierarchies of the medieval world, the conviction grew that the least government was best. Americans in general are concerned about the ever-growing size and influence of government, and they are reluctant to allow it to focus its authority. Keep it separated, checked, and balanced, and don't let it plan, particularly in Washington, D.C. Let it be responsive to crisis and to interest groups. Whoever pays the price can call the tune. Says Huntington: "Because of the inherently antigovernment character of the American Creed, government that is strong is illegitimate, government that is legitimate is weak."[8]

5. *Scientific specialization*. This is the corruption of Newtonian mechanics, which says that if we attend to the parts, as experts, specialists, and academics, the whole will take care of itself. From its inception as a nation America has strayed from these ideas to cope with reality—economic depressions, competing global systems, urban concentration, ecological disasters and, most recently, terrorism. Nevertheless, as we have said, these ideas retain great resilience and retain the hallmark of legitimacy. Two difficulties result. First, the old ideas perform less well

as definitions of values—for example, justice, economy—in the real
world of today. Second, many important institutions, including great
corporations and national governments, have radically departed from
the old ideology in the name of efficiency, economies of scale, productivity, human rights, welfare, and the environment without appreciating
the ideological consequences of their departure.

To take but one example: foreigners often complain that Americans
preach the old ideas abroad even while they practice something quite
different at home. Free trade is a well-known example. In 1997 in Kazakhstan, one of the authors observed U.S. and World Bank economists
cautioning the new post-Soviet government against intervening to help
restart agriculture after the end of Soviet rule. The experts argued that
farmers should be endowed with property and then left to compete in
an open market. This policy prescription failed to mention that the
United States—and virtually every other rich country—had abandoned
such practice long ago, favoring instead generous assistance to agriculture of every kind, including export and production subsidies and im-
port tariff and quota protection. This example from Kazakhstan to
which we shall return in a later chapter represented a remarkable but
not uncommon gap between theory and practice.

Consider, too, the effects of the second difficulty, namely ignoring
the consequences of departure from the ideology. We mention below
the U.S. government's promise of a "right to a job" for all Americans—
and there are a variety of other promised rights including, for example,
a right to high-quality health care for all Americans. In establishing
these rights, however, the government failed to see the inevitable costly
and politically controversial consequences: if the state guaranteed rights,
it had to and eventually would prescribe duties—a duty to work (welfare
reform), for example, or an obligation to avoid unhealthy practices such
as smoking or overeating.

Another example is the extraordinary growth of the modern corporation. Corporations have employed the power of government, often in a
kind of partnership, to promote their interests which are held to be the
same as those of the public in general. President Richard Nixon reliev-
ing ITT of antitrust prosecution (see page 34) in the name of a healthy
U.S. economy exemplifies this, as does the close relationship between
government and such industries as pharmaceuticals and defense. This

type of cooperation between big business and an active, planning state may be fine as long as the rules that govern it are clear.

Shifting from individualism, if we were to ask then what ideology *would* legitimize the actual behavior of U.S. business and government, we would come up with five counterparts to the Lockean ideas called communitarianism. And if we were to speculate about what eventually might be a global ideology, one within which many different local versions might fit, communitarianism could well describe it. This is not surprising, since if we look beyond the West—Britain and America really—to most of Europe, the Middle East, Africa, and Asia, the dominant ideology has always been some form of communitarianism, sometimes brutal as in the old USSR but often humane as in Japan and Singapore.

Here then is the alternative to individualism that seems to fit institutional behavior in the United States and elsewhere, again naming it after its first component.

1. *Communitarianism.* The community is more than the sum of the individuals in it. It is organic, not atomistic. It has special and urgent needs as a community. The survival and self-respect of the individuals in it depend on the recognition of those needs. If the community—the workplace or the neighborhood—is well designed, its members will have a sense of identity with it. They will be able to make maximum use of their capacities. If it is poorly designed, they will be alienated and frustrated.

*Equality of result.* There has been a shift in the notion of equality. Under the original idea of equality of opportunity, blacks, whites, men, and women had equal places at the starting line and each was supposed to be able to go as far as he or she was able without discriminatory obstruction. Some thirty years ago the U.S. Congress decided that the idea was not producing the results it wanted. The starting line was bent, it said, and obstructions abounded. The law was changed. "Affirmative action" was ushered in. AT&T, at the time the largest employer in America, was found guilty of "systemic" discrimination because it had only female telephone operators, only male vice presidents, and minority groups at the bottom of the pay scale. The company, supposing that its personnel policies had been exemplary, was shocked. Women liked to be telephone operators, it told the government. Men like to be vice presidents, and minority group members were happy to be hired at all. The government replied that it had no interest in what individuals might like. It wanted to see a certain overall corporate profile: male telephone operators, female vice presidents, and minority groups spread up and down the pay scale in proportion to their numbers in the surrounding community—in short, equality of result.

The government's action caused great concern and confusion at AT&T. Many argued for waiting until the community recovered its senses and returned to the old idea of equality of opportunity—not result. The more hardheaded, however, saw that the only real choice the company had was how to implement the new idea with a minimum of waste and hardship. This the company did with great skill—recruiting, training, motivating, and placing so as to make the best of it.

The "crisis" in this case was the growing awareness by the public of the gross inequities being suffered by women and minorities in America. The task facing AT&T's managers was how to make maximum use of minimum crisis for maximum change—in other words, how to make every bit of crisis count. To do this required an inspection of their ideological assumptions and then an evaluation of their reliability. Doing so, managers—often reluctantly—decided that the old ideas, the old justifications, would not stand up against the onslaught of interest groups, legislatures, and courts. They had to change.

Affirmative action has been under attack since its inception by those who argue that it is incompatible with individualism (equality of opportunity). Many attempts have been made to turn back the clock, but most have failed. AT&T and other big employers, once having changed, see it as next to impossible to go back. Thus, when an ideology is changed in practice the community might revere the old idea, but it does not return to it.

Before leaving this slot in the ideological framework, it is worth noting that in some communities—historically as well as today—the idea of *equality* is replaced by that of *hierarchy*. In feudal times it was the notion of class. In modern Japan it is the idea of merit: your place in society is determined by a sequence of rigorous examinations with the elite being the summa cum laude graduates from the University of Tokyo.

*Consensus.* Contracts, of course, still exist, but in many relationships—buyers and sellers, employees and employers, and even husbands and wives—consensus has come to be both a more efficient and a more reliable basis for proceeding.

Let us look at labor relations, for example. In the nineteenth century the contract was an individualistic device to connect the manager/owner to the worker and it was hierarchical in nature: the manager hired and decided the terms of employment which the worker could accept or reject. The real world being what it was, the worker was inclined to accept, the alternative being grim. With the rise of trade unions, the contract became collectivized and adversarial, an ideological horror for many employers. Over time the collective contract and the bargaining that went with it became cumbersome, time-consuming, and uncompetitive compared with more consensual ways such as those characteristic of Japan. So practices changed. Toyota actually took over General Motors' plant in Fremont, California, to show GM and the United Automobile Workers how to manage the transition. "Workers" became "team members" and the managers' job was to support the team.

In Europe in the 1970s the new arrangements were called industrial democracy, co-determination, workers' councils, and the like. In the United States the transition had a number of headings: organizational development, job enrichment, and quality of work-life programs. In both places the transition has been impeded by the residue of old ideology. Trade unions were reluctant to shed the power and authority that came with the old idea of contract. Managers also were nervous about moving away from their old bases of authority. If improved productivity and competitiveness depend upon the transition, the issue is clear: how much crisis was required, how much recession before Europe and America revived. MNCs, of course, can move abroad to avoid the problems at home, leaving trade unions and the old ways to wither, as is occurring in many countries.

The problem for the manager of a giant multinational corporation is that none of these transitional forces is working very well. So NGOs, as we will discuss at greater length later, have moved in to fill the vacuum. Some try to use "shareholder democracy" as a vehicle for control. Others work among the managed or try to make use of national govern-

Box 2.1

**The Tata Group of India**

The Tata Group of India, a family conglomerate, is India's largest company, with $17.5 billion in revenues and $1.9 billion in profits during the twelve months preceding March 2005. The 131-year-old company has always conceived its purpose as being the development of India as an industrial power, and, according to *Newsweek International*, "66 percent of the profits of its highly successful arm, Tata Sons, go to charity."

In recent years, Tata has gone global, acquiring Tetley Tea in Britain, Daewoo Motors in South Korea, and NatSteel in Singapore. It has also moved into markets where many MNCs "fear to tread" in Bangladesh and Africa, regarding itself as a "for-profit development agency," building schools and hospitals, and training carpenters, electricians, mechanics, and other skilled workers.

SOURCE: George Wehrfritz and Ron Moreau, "A New Kind of Company," *Newsweek International*, June 5, 2005, pp. 10–12.

ments and intergovernmental organizations such as the World Trade Organization. And some take direct action of one sort or another.

One promising model of a communitarian multinational is the Tata Group of India that *Newsweek International* has hailed as "the hot newcomer in the global economy"[9] (see box 2.1). Its consensual relationship with its workers, forged over many years with a powerful union, has, for example, made Tata Steel the low-cost competitor in India's steel industry. Tata's car plant at Pune has gone sixteen years without a work stoppage, and the local union representative, Sujit Patil, says his people work closely with management every day—a state of labor relations that he said was "very different" from that at other Indian companies.

2. *Rights and duties of membership.* Property rights have lost their sacred status and become one of a number of rights of membership. For

a century or more in America and elsewhere, a different set of rights has been surpassing property rights in political and social importance. These are, for example, rights to income, pensions, health care, and other entitlements associated with membership in the community. Frequently, corporations are the instruments through which these communitarian rights are provided. Even if one doesn't own a thing, these rights are guarantees of a safe place in society.

Escalating rights have strained the ability of governments to pay for them and emphasized the fact that if the community provides its members with rights it must and inevitably will prescribe duties. This raises the controversial question: Who decides an individual's duty? In Japan, Korea, and some other Asian countries, according to traditional ideology the community imposes duties and generally they are weighted more heavily than rights. But in the United States and perhaps the West generally, so-called liberals and conservatives alike have been inclined to leave the question of duty to the individual—to upbringing, religion, and conscience. The inexorabilities of communitarianism, however, are forcing governments to define the duty of those who do not seem to be doing it for themselves. If everyone has a right to a job, as the Humphrey-Hawkins Act suggests for the United States, does not everyone who is able-bodied have a duty to work? If so, how is that idea implemented? There would seem to be three ways of dealing with the idle: government can pay them; government can employ them; or government can coerce and subsidize business to employ them. Europe and the United States, it would seem, tend to prefer the first two, Japan and China the third.

In the face of growing divergence of income and wealth in some countries, such as the United States, Sierra Leone, and Brazil, the question arises: If the duties of the poor and the weak are to be made more explicit (as in "welfare reform"), does it not follow that the duties of the rich and powerful (i.e., corporate CEOs) must also be made clear? And what is the relevant community for thinking about rights and duties? Is it the nation or a region such as the EU or, given the concern with poverty reduction in developing countries, is it not becoming the world? If so, who decides global rights and duties? The great MNCs are perceived by many today as being the decision-makers, but by what right do they decide such life and death questions? Some say "the market" decides, but the protesters outside the meeting halls of the rich object that the market is unjust. Ideological analysis helps us to see the questions even if it may not provide the answers.

Not only have membership rights become more important than property rights, but the utility of property as a legitimizing idea has eroded. As we mentioned earlier, it is hard to define large public corporations as private property at all. The half-million shareholders of General Motors do not and cannot control or in any sense be responsible for "their" property. Furthermore, the vast majority of them have no desire for such responsibility. Attempts at "shareholder democracy" have done little to deal with the problem. The fact is that GM and the thousands of companies like it are collectives floating in philosophic limbo, dangerously vulnerable to the charge of illegitimacy and to the charge that they are beyond community control.

Consider how the management of this nonproprietary institution is selected. The myth, rooted in the old ideology, is that stockholders select the board of directors, which, in turn, selects the management. Usually, however, this is not true. The management selects the board and the board, generally speaking, blesses the management in return for generous fees. Managers thus get to be managers through some mystical hierarchical process of questionable legitimacy.[10]

The scale of executive compensation is a good example of how illegitimacy springs from ideological confusion. Theoretically the shareholders determine managers' pay, but in fact of course they can't and don't. Employing the communitarian idea of rights and duties of membership as a way of thinking about what is fair and legitimate would doubtless cause a reduction in executive compensation from what it is today. A *Business Week* survey in 2000, for example, showed that the average U.S. workers' weekly pay in 1998 was 12 percent below the 1973 level (adjusted for inflation) despite a 33 percent increase in worker productivity in the same period, whereas the CEOs of the companies surveyed enjoyed a 36 percent pay hike.[11] Neva Goodwin of Tufts University has estimated that in 1998 the compensation of top CEOs was "nearly ten thousand times the hourly rate of the average production worker," a difference that strikes some as illegitimate.[12]

The full solution of the current corporate governance problems has been set aside because of the power of the old ideology, the difficulty of arranging a new one, and the undoubted effectiveness of the current corporate form. In the past, when economic growth and progress were wholly synonymous, the United States and other industrial countries preferred to leave managers as free as possible from stockholder interference in the name of efficiency. But today the definition of efficiency, the criteria for measuring economic growth, and the effects of growth are far less certain. So sticking with the myth of the corporation as property as a passport to legitimacy has become increasingly precarious. Consequently, a plethora of other means, not all efficient or effective, has emerged to legitimize the large corporation. These include regulation by the nation-state, by regions of nation-states such as the European Union, or by global institutions that states create such as the World Trade Organization. There has also been an extraordinary proliferation of an increasingly clamorous body of NGOs and efforts by coalitions of corporations themselves: for example, the chemical industry's initiative to ban the use of ozone-depleting chlorofluorocarbons (CFCs).

American MNCs in collaboration with the U.S. government have sought to impose the idea of property rights on the rest of the world in such industries as biotechnology, drugs, software manufacture, movies, and music. When it comes to the protection of patents in pharmaceuticals the world has objected, arguing that the right to property is not absolute. More important is a right of membership existing alongside other rights, to health, for example.[13] People in the developed world, of course, are also clamoring for improved property rights, to land in particular, as a way of lifting themselves out of poverty through better access to credit and transactions as a result of a secure land title.[14]

3. *Community need.* The old idea was that competition among self-interested proprietors to satisfy consumer desires in the marketplace would produce a good community and that the sum of consumer desires would equal community need. This has lost some force. For example, an *Economist* survey of corporate social responsibility reported, "It would be a challenge to find a recent annual report of any big international company that justifies the firm's existence merely in terms of profit, rather than 'service to the community.' . . . Big firms nowadays are called upon to be good corporate citizens. And they all want to show they are."[15]

Market competition is indeed wonderfully efficient, as Adam Smith observed, but without an efficient, honest, and responsive government it sometimes fails to meet community needs in relation to, for example, clean air and water, and poverty reduction. Such needs can also include more nebulous items. For centuries Kazakhstan had a flourishing traditional cottage textile industry. After the breakup of the USSR, Western economists, as a precondition to providing financial assistance, forced the country to lower all tariffs in order to "free" the market so that the preferred idea could work. Within months there were no more cottage textile industries.

On a somewhat grander scale it was to the notion of community need, that is, the national interest in global competitiveness, to which ITT appealed in 1971 when it sought to prevent the U.S. Justice Department from divesting it of Hartford Fire Insurance. (The department's antitrust division argued that the huge size of the company threatened to contaminate the market.) The company lawyers said, in effect: Don't visit that old idea of marketplace competition on us; the public interest requires ITT to be big and strong so that it can compete in the world and return $6 billion a year to the U.S. balance of payments (which was just moving into a prolonged deficit at that time). As is often the case, here the company was arguing the radical, that is, communitarian, case. The suggestion was obvious: ITT was a partner with government in both defining and implementing the national interest. There might have been some doubt about who was the senior partner, but partnership it was. This concept is radically different from that underlying the antitrust laws, namely, that the public interest emerges *naturally* from free and vigorous competition among numerous aggressive, individualistic, and preferably small companies attempting to satisfy consumer desires.

There are, after all, only four ways in which business activity can be harmonized with community need:

  (i) competition to satisfy consumer desires;
  (ii) government regulation;
  (iii) partnership between government and business (as in the defense industry); and
  (iv) the corporate charter through which government gives business its license to exist.

Competition will surely continue; it is indeed often the most efficient route to fulfilling many community needs. But the other routes are essential where it fails, and here the question is: what is the relevant mechanism for assessing community needs in 2004? Is it the nation, the region? Is it not the world? If so, who decides the world's needs? Is it business in the marketplace? Or NGOs? Or governments?

4. *Active, planning state.* The prodigious power of the old antigovernment idea in the United States is surely revealed in the promise of every president of recent memory to reduce its size and "get it off our backs." And the equally impressive force of the communitarian reality is evident in their failure to do so. President George W. Bush, among the more emphatic devotees of the waning individualistic ideology, has stunned his like-minded followers with his big government agenda. While endorsing unprecedented invasion of individual civil rights by the Justice Department, Bush has created the biggest new bureaucracy since Harry Truman, the Department of Homeland Security; pushed the powers of the federal government into education and abortion rights, hitherto state responsibilities; proposed a national energy policy to reduce dependence on foreign oil; slapped protective barriers on steel; signed a farm bill costing $180 billion over ten years; and set up a White House office to promote marriage. In its first three years the Bush administration increased federal spending by 21 percent. "Appalling," said Ed Crane, head of the Cato Institute, a Lockean think tank.[16]

It is hard to think of a better example of how a manager, in this case the U.S. president, subverts his own legitimacy by preaching what he does not and cannot, and maybe even should not, practice.

Great corporations recognize both the urgency of obtaining a reliable definition of community need—what's safe, what's clean, and so forth—and also, unlike the businessman on the Nashua River to whom we referred earlier, the fact that sooner or later government will be the definer of those needs and the enforcer of policies to meet them. Thus, for example, after some delays, the large U.S. chemical companies came to work closely with the Environmental Protection Agency to enforce the Toxic Substances Control Act and other such legislation. This partnership is suspect in some quarters because of doubts about who the senior partner is, but it is nevertheless a necessity for both sides if the environment is to be safeguarded.

Increasingly, ecological hazards such as climate change transcend national boundaries. This once again raises the issue of what is the relevant community when defining needs and increasingly the answer is extranational bodies, although the world as yet has no real government to make such definitions.

Globalization, characterized by vastly increased flows of trade and capital managed by MNCs, has clearly diminished the power of the state to control its jurisdiction. This is true not only for weak states but even for the most powerful. China has become the largest creditor of the United States, financing a U.S. current account deficit that is currently about 6 percent of GDP. At the same time, however, globalization has enhanced the importance of the state in planning its strategy to compete in the world. It is worth remembering that the most successful economies in the years since the end of World War II have been those in which the state has played a critical role in organizing national resources: Japan, South Korea, Singapore, Taiwan, and China. Even in the United States, for all its Lockean pretensions, the U.S. government's Defense Advanced Research Agency (DARPA) must be credited not only with the invention of the Internet but with the coordination of industry, academia, and venture capital so as to create many of the high-tech innovations of the last forty years.

5. *Holism, interdependence.* Finally, and perhaps most fundamentally, the old idea of scientific specialization, which remains the bedrock of our educational institutions, has given way to a new consciousness of the interrelatedness of all things. Spaceship earth, our life-supporting biosphere, and globalization have dramatized the fact that everything is related to everything else.

Do managers scan the environment in a specialized way, as has been the scientific tradition embalmed in the disciplines of academia, or do they seek to grasp the wholes that are there, looking for the systemic relations that compose reality? If they do the latter they will find themselves bereft of experts and very much on their own. Specialists are, of course, necessary, but their utility will increasingly depend on their being managed by those with a holistic consciousness.

Old ideologies do not die. Individualism will live forever, but it is becoming part of a communitarian amalgam. This is not necessarily good; it is just inevitable, and we must deal with it. Communitarianism, we know, may threaten the liberty and individual rights for which many have bled and died. Communitarianism need not be totalitarian, but it could be. It need not lead to inhuman bureaucratic centralization, but it might. It does not necessarily foster an excess of nationalism, but again it could. So, as we travel down this path let us hope that managers of the world's largest companies will have the insight and vision to make the best of it.

There will, of course, never be a single world ideology. There will be as many ideologies as there are communities, but given the way the world is going there is clearly convergence around a communitarian theme. Communitarianism will be the language in which differences in the business world can be fruitfully discussed, and indeed it is the language of many corporate leaders to whom we shall refer in the chapters that follow. Managers everywhere can more realistically anticipate and manage the future if they can understand and speak that language.

## Historical Roots—Capitalism or What?

Mainstream economists have not been too helpful in answering this question. Many of them remain in the embrace of Adam Smith, for whom competition among self-interested proprietors to satisfy consumers in an open marketplace would, through the workings of an "invisible hand," result in the good community with the least government being considered the best.

These economists, like Smith and Locke before them, find this theory to be "natural," that is, to spring from human nature and the natural order of things. And it is universal: communities that do not conform to the theory are "unnatural" deviations from the norm. As the historian Geoffrey Hodgson notes in his insightful book, *How Economics Forgot History: The Problem of Historical Specificity in Social Science*, for many professional economists free markets are indeed the ideal. If the reality does not fit the theory, "the reality must be made to fit the theory." Under such circumstances, writes Hodgson, "economics becomes the study of one ideal, a pure market system," all others being an aberration from the "ideal norm." He points out that the post–World War II success of the United States bolstered this approach, even though the country often failed to practice the theory its economists preached. (Indeed, until the 1930s the United States was one of the most protectionist countries in the world.)

What happens when there is no market, as was the case in ex-Soviet countries? Hodgson quotes the economist Ronald Coase: "The ex-Communist countries are advised to move to a market economy . . . but without the appropriate institutions, no market of any significance is possible."[17] Nevertheless, the theory, rooted as it is in capitalism as individualism, thrives even today in the so-called Washington consensus. Its high priests are a collection of economists in the U.S. Treasury, the World Bank, the International Monetary Fund, and elsewhere who for much of recent history have sought to impose a one-size-fits-all, free-market system on every community everywhere, whatever the local reality might be. Inevitably, their ideology is eroding as it fails to adapt to the real world, but a distressing amount of crisis has been required to foment a transition. Today we see signs that the adherents of the Washington Consensus are finally beginning to accept that there is no single template model to achieve economic development. Thankfully, "clinical economics," as Jeffery Sachs calls it, the tailoring of specific economic policy solutions to country-specific economic policy problems, is gaining sway.

This view—that the tenets of individualistic capitalism need some tenderizing—is certainly widespread in historical practice. As Thomas K. McCraw of Harvard Business School has pointed out, Alexander Hamilton, Frederich List, and (somewhat later) the Japanese developed a different theory of economic development centered on a nationalistic, mercantilist nation-state focused not on the consumer in the marketplace but on the producer and the organizations that the producer manages. Their theory entails a very different view of markets, property, and government than that espoused by the followers of Adam Smith. If the economy and the political surroundings envisaged by Smith define "capitalism," then what Hamilton and List advocated, and the Japanese,

Koreans, and Taiwanese have adopted, is surely not capitalism. But then, of course, neither is it socialism.[18]

Capitalism as individualism has been further undermined by other phenomena—poverty, hunger, disparities between rich and poor, and environmental degradation. Consequently, Sir Geoffrey Owen, Senior Fellow at the London School of Economics, speaks of "a new way of thinking about the functions and duties of the modern corporation . . ., which puts much less weight on the sovereignty of shareholders and much more on the responsibility of corporate managers to serve the needs of society at large."[19]

As we have noted, the question of course arises: What are those needs and who decides? The conventional notion that governments decide is not entirely satisfying for a rising tide of NGOs. They observe that a number of poor countries have unreliable governments that are unwilling or unable to address the problems of poverty in their midst. NGOs further protest that even the governments of the world's strong and stable democracies cannot be counted on to decide community need correctly. And increasingly the most enlightened corporate leaders are singing the same tune. For example, in 2000 Sir Mark Moody-Stuart, then chairman of Shell International Petroleum, wrote on behalf of Shell: "Because we too are concerned at the requirement to address those in poverty who are excluded from the benefits that many of us share in the global economy, we share the objective of the recent demonstrators in Seattle, Davos and Prague."[20]

Leaders of the corporate social responsibility (CSR) movement embrace the idea of "corporate citizenship" and pledge their companies to meet the needs of the communities they affect. The global manufacturing company ABB of Switzerland, for example, says in *A Brief Guide to ABB* that the mission of the company is "to create value" for a number of "stakeholders," adding: "For the communities where we operate and for society at large, we create value by living our commitment to sustainable development."[21] This type of communitarian commitment is typical of the commitment espoused by the 160 corporate members of the World Business Council for Sustainable Development, about which we will say more later.

This sort of corporate approach sidesteps Milton Friedman's warning to corporations to eschew any "social responsibility other than to make as much money for the shareholders as possible."[22] Farsighted managers have recognized that the source of their legitimacy has moved, and that alongside shareholder satisfaction and marketplace competition has come the servicing of community needs, however they might be defined. If governments are unable or unwilling to define community needs within their jurisdiction and if there is no government to do so for the world, then corporations must do it with the help of NGOs, self-appointed groups often with strong feelings about what the world needs. This is not to say that Friedman is fully debunked, merely that the long-run means to profit has changed. Also, corporations know that distrust of the profit motive is on the rise. Here are the words of some of the world's most distinguished business leaders. In a book entitled *Walking the Talk*, Charles O. Holliday, Jr., CEO of Dupont; Stephan Schmidheiny, chairman of Anova Holding AG; and Philip Watts, former chairman of the Committee of Managing Directors of the Royal Dutch Shell Group, wrote:

> Companies need to design and implement ways for markets to bridge the "affordability gap," reaching people in areas where ordinary business models do not work. . . . Business is becoming more interested in working to develop partnerships with governments and civil society (NGOs) to demonstrate that markets can help people toward sustainable livelihoods. The business case for poverty reduction is straightforward. Business cannot succeed in societies that fail. Poverty wastes human resources—the ability of the poor to contribute to societal development.[23]

The authors praised Unilever for "exploring the power of public-private partnerships in helping to tackle sustainable development challenges in Africa." Unilever's tackling of a broad range of development challenges in Bangladesh is another excellent example. Other leading business executives have been quoted on the topic as well. As Richard George, CEO of the Canadian electric utility Suncor Energy, noted: "All citizens of the world desire clean air, clean water, and healthy, natural ecosystems. However, before we can aspire to assure this environmental future for all citizens, we need to tackle the problems of global poverty." John Pepper, chairman of Procter & Gamble, added: "We cannot condemn developing countries to a life of poverty

so those in the developed world can maintain their lifestyles." And
Peter Sutherland, chairman of BP in 1999, stated that "eliminating
poverty is not only the right thing to do; it is essential to fulfilling the
world's growth potential."[24]

The leaders of great multinationals in the spirit of communitarianism
are eloquent in their commitment to serving community needs and
many try to do so, often in partnership with NGOs and government.
The results, however, are disappointing because an effective organizational mechanism, and reward for their efforts in the form of increased
profits, successful examples, and strengthened legitimacy, are lacking.

# PART II

## Reactions, Responses, and Responsibilities

# NGOs and the Attack:
# Critics, Watchdogs, and Collaborators

As the old ideas concerning corporate legitimacy erode, various players are moving to define and give institutional vitality to the new ones. They are encouraging, assisting, and pressuring corporations to increase globalization's benefits and diminish its costs. Among other things, they seek to increase and improve the contribution that MNCs make to the reduction of global poverty. The players constitute the international development architecture, and we shall observe that that architecture contains a large and important gap that needs to be filled.

In the next three chapters we describe this architecture and give brief synopses of the players and their dynamics, and a definition of the gap. There are the nongovernmental organizations that attack, cajole, criticize, and monitor, as well as collaborate with the MNCs. Then there are the MNCs themselves, which are often seeking better methods of relating to the communities they affect, sometimes joining with NGOs. Finally, there are the governmental and intergovernmental organizations and agencies concerned with poverty reduction and development. Although we separate these organizations for purposes of description, they are, of course, tied together and are in many ways reflections of one another.

This chapter focuses specifically on NGOs and their role in determining the course of events that has afflicted MNCs and compromised their legitimacy. Although sometimes characterized as troublemakers, their centrality to the evolving nature of MNCs is growing stronger. The style of NGO interaction with MNCs has changed over time: these days, as we shall see, NGOs often work together closely with MNCs. Nevertheless, for the most part, NGOs and MNCs almost invariably regard each other as adversaries.

Attacks by NGOs mostly center on the corporation's impact on human rights and the natural environment, included under numbers two, three, and five in the communitarian framework cited in chapter 2; that is, rights of membership, community need, and holism. What NGOs mean by human rights is set out in the Charter of Human Rights of the United Nations, conventions of the International Labor Organizations, and international law: these form the basis of world public opinion. They include prohibition of child labor, the right to a decent wage and safe working conditions, and the right of employees to organize into unions. Several companies are being taken to U.S. courts under the Alien Tort Claims Act (ATCA), charged with torture and murder in countries such as Indonesia and Sudan, and many companies are attacked for despoiling the environment: polluting the air and water, destroying the forests, and adversely affecting the climate. The prosecution is led by NGOs, sometimes called civil society organizations (CSOs), which constitute an increasingly powerful global network of what some have termed vigilantes.[1] Among the techniques they employ to harass and punish wrongdoers are consumer boycotts, shareholder protests, and publicity aimed at fouling the names and images of offending corporations and shaming their managers. Sometimes NGOs use the machinery of established governments to do what the governments themselves cannot or will not do. They also play an increasingly influential role in the operations of intergovernmental bodies such as the United Nations and World Bank. And they are big. In the 1990s, lending by the World Bank averaged about $20 billion per year; by 1994 NGOs were funneling about $8 billion per year into developing countries.[2] Moreover, the number of operational NGOs continues to rise.

According to Michael Edwards of the Ford Foundation, more than 40,000 international NGOs are now in operation around the world, more than 90 percent of them formed since 1970.[3] Edwards reported, for example, that "the number of registered NGOs in Nepal increased from 220 in 1990 to 1,210 in 1993; in Bolivia from 100 in 1980 to 530 in 1992; and in Tunisia from 1,886 in 1988 to 5,186 in 1991."[4] Membership in NGOs has also risen dramatically.

Although perhaps as many as six thousand NGOs are of the attacking variety, most are not. The Bangladesh Rural Advancement

Committee (BRAC), for example, now provides services to two million people. Other well-known international NGOs that have seen membership climb include: Sierra Club (114,000 in 1970 to 550,000 in 1996); Greenpeace (250 in 1971 to 1.7 million in 1996); and Amnesty International (39,000 in 1987 to 108,000 in 1992).[5] It is important to note that although the number and coverage of NGOs has grown rapidly, only a handful of major NGOs control the lion's share of resources and have a sizable membership base. By the late 1990s, eight internationally operating NGOs, including CARE, Oxfam, World Vision, and Medicins Sans Frontieres, implemented about half of the global budget of more than $8 billion for humanitarian relief work.[6] Yet when outsiders hear the umbrella term "NGO," they do not tend to think of variegated forms of stylized NGOs, but rather consider them all of roughly the same ilk.

## The Attackers

For most MNC managers the term NGO conjures a threatening image. They feel unsure how to respond when confronted with criticism or challenge from an NGO. An NGO will play on a manager's fears, alleging perhaps that the MNC is not doing the "right thing" by its staff in Mozambique, for example, or is ultimately responsible for misplaced or misspent tax dollars previously paid to the recognized government of Yemen. The complaint will often have nothing to do with an infringement of the law. The MNC manager is therefore understandably uncertain how to respond. But he or she knows—and recent experience confirms—that an inappropriate response can carry serious adverse consequences for the business.

There was a time not too long ago when the legitimacy of a global corporation was largely a matter of obeying the law as it was promulgated and enforced by the state. This is no longer the case. And in many countries—developing countries especially—the local governments, in the eyes of the NGOs and the world opinion that sustains them, are too weak, ineffectual, or corrupt to be trusted. Indeed, some of the oil companies that are defendants in ATCA suits are accused of conspiring with local governments to torture and kill. Speaking ideologically, the

"active, planning state" is either unable, unwilling, or finds it unaccept-
able to do what it is supposed to do in the community—define rights
and community needs and ensure that they are provided. This is all part
of a slippage in the sovereignty of the nation-state, to which Kofi Annan
alluded when he spoke of the UN having a mandate not from governments but from "the peoples" based on principles of human rights rather
than legal definitions of the nation-state.[7] There is thus an enormous
governance vacuum that the vigilantes are eager to fill.[8]

Harvard University's John Ruggie, an expert in this field, has written
of "the emergence of what we might call a global public domain: an
arena of discourse, contestation and action organized around global
rule-making—a transnational space that is not exclusively inhabited by
states, and which permits the direct expression and pursuit of human
interests, not merely those mandated by the state." He cites civil society
organizations (or NGOs) acting upon "the global corporate sector" as
"one of the major drivers" of this expression and pursuit.[9]

We can conclude that NGOs attack corporations for several reasons.

(i) Corporations have done bad things and thus need watching.
(ii) Corporations are the most important vehicle for improving
the lives of the poor in the world and thus need to be prodded
to make full use of their potential.
(iii) Corporations are vulnerable.

A 1999 study by the United Nations Research Institute for Social
Development, which was rather ahead of its time, examined the consequences of the new trend in NGOs' influence over corporations and
the consequent responses by the latter.[10] The study referred to this trend
as "civil regulation." It concluded that, in a globalizing economy, civil
regulation by NGOs would be the chief driver of corporate social and
environmental responsibility. "Through the politics of both pressure and
engagement, NGOs are creating the new agenda for business as much
as companies are themselves."[11]

Faced with these exogenous pressures and existing in the philosophic
limbo that we described earlier, MNCs cannot take their legitimacy for
granted. Generally, attacks on an MNC are led by a consortium of
NGOs rather than any single organization. In many cases, the consor-

tium is not formally initiated but often organically grows out of a tacit consensus about objectives. Examples include consortium NGO attacks on Shell's activities in the North Sea and Nigeria, with Greenpeace among the most vocal; attacks on McDonald's Restaurants' global operations by cultural and health-related NGOs or by a single individual such as the producer of the recent documentary movie *Super Size Me*; attacks on Nike and Levi Strauss by NGOs concerned with human rights; and attacks on Phillip Morris for promoting smoking, especially in poor countries. Forms of attack include consumer boycotts, mailings to financiers and shareholders, and blockades of company facilities.

Another example is the Rainforest Action Network that forced Citigroup to adopt policies to reduce habitat loss and global warming. It urged customers to cut up their Citicards and loaded the Internet with what *The Economist* called "nasty jibes against named executives." Employee morale suffered. Matt Arnold, a Harvard MBA and Greenpeace veteran who worked out a truce, said that Citigroup executives hated being bullied and heckled. In April 2003, RAN announced that the financial giant had agreed to do what it wanted. "Not bad for a group with a dozen staff and a $2 million budget."[12]

Furthermore, NGOs believe, with some justification according to a study by Professor Andrew Walter of the London School of Economics, that corporate lobby groups have captured government policies regarding international property rights such as those of the United States.[13] NGOs certainly thought this to be the case in the mid-1990s when they worked to thwart efforts by the Organization for European Cooperation and Development to create the Multilateral Agreement on Investment, an international umbrella framework to govern foreign direct investment.[14] NGOs opposed the MAI because they felt that large corporations had captured the negotiating agenda and that the governments of developing countries would be handicapped in the debate over the terms of the agreement. The MAI incident reveals that big business does not stand alone as a target of NGO animosity; governmental institutions such as the OECD and, as we shall see in chapter 5, the United Nations are also mistrusted. A brief synopsis of the collapse of earlier plans to bring the MAI into existence is given in box 3.1.

The attack on the apparel industry—on Nike, Reebok, The Gap, and Wal-Mart, among others—has been especially spectacular because

Box 3.1

### OECD's Multicultural Agreement on Investment: Dissent and Demise

The opposition by NGOs to the MAI in the mid-1990s occurred before the NGO movement really hit its stride in opposition to globalization during the world trade talks in Seattle in 1999. Moreover, the MAI negotiations were being conducted by the OECD rather than the World Trade Organization, the former considered by MAI backers to be much less of a lightning rod for NGO criticism than the latter.

The backers of the MAI saw it as a rather benign formalization and unification of the scores of existing bilateral treaties relating to investment and really nothing more than a mirror of the international regimes that already governed trade. This view was not shared by NGOs that regarded the MAI as one more step in the process of globalization that they opposed and, as if by magic, a diverse coalition of NGOs coalesced to kill it. OECD member countries eventually shelved the initiative.

SOURCE: Involved policy-makers and Andrew Walter, "NGOs, Business and International Investment: the Multilateral Agreement on Investment, Seattle, and Beyond," *Global Governance* (January–March, 2001).

of the grim reality that the anti-sweatshop activists have exposed in the apparel factories of the poor world that supply the big-name companies with their products. More than forty different groups of NGOs were involved and the industry was highly vulnerable to consumer boycotts. When the issue made headlines in 1996, President Clinton led the formation of an Apparel Industry Partnership to fight sweatshops internationally. In 1998, the AIP created a Fair Labor Association to oversee implementation and monitoring of an agreed-upon code of conduct. At the same time the Council on Economic Priorities, a venerable and respected NGO, worked with companies and unions to establish a stricter and more far-reaching code, SA8000, promulgated by Social

Accountability International, a CEP subsidiary. Details of the deployment of SA8000 can be found in the next chapter.

In 2004 the NGO, People for the Ethical Treatment of Animals, threatened U.S. clothing retailers that used Australian wool in their production. (Box 3.2 details the relevant events and claims.) In short, PETA was opposed to wool production techniques used by the Australian wool industry, the world's largest producer, and threatened to launch a major negative advertising campaign against major U.S. clothing retailers that did not cease the purchase of Australian wool. PETA provided samples of the planned critical advertisements to let the corporations know it was serious. One advertisement targeted the large U.S. clothing retailer Abercrombie & Fitch, which eventually yielded to the threat even though it reportedly was not even a buyer of Australian wool. Some might describe this process as extortion. Certainly those in the Australian wool production business did. The Australian wool industry responded through the media that, as the world's largest and most sophisticated producer of wool, it was at the forefront of sustainable and humane wool production practices and followed every relevant law, not to mention additional requirements of other groups such as the Royal Society for Prevention of Cruelty to Animals (RSPCA). The Australian wool industry came to view PETA as a collection of thugs operating extra-legally.

NGOs in general seek to influence or oppose the behavior of MNCs. Some are more focused on broader development issues, some on specific issues. Some are more interested in advocacy than others. Greenpeace, Transparency International, and Oxfam are examples of well-known NGOs that influence community thinking, often through the media, sending messages that are carefully watched and interpreted by MNCs. Sometimes NGOs push for changes in the behavior of MNCs in developing countries: for more effort, or less impact, or wider distribution of benefits, or better conditions. Sometimes these requests gather enough traction to cause lawmakers to adopt their agendas. And sometimes they don't, leaving MNCs uncertain about what the "community need" is to which they are supposed to respond and how they are supposed to do so.

Increasingly, it is the staff of major corporations who, personally identifying with some of the transmitted signals from NGOs and other parts

## Box 3.2

### Abercrombie & Fitch and the Attack by PETA

In October 2004 the U.S.-based NGO, People for the Ethical Treatment of Animals (PETA), demanded that Abercrombie & Fitch, a large retail fashion brand in the United States with sales over $1 billion per annum, boycott the purchase of wool from Australia for use in the production of clothing sold in its stores. PETA, which was also targeting other U.S.-based clothing retailers in relation to the purchase of Australian wool, was threatening to launch a media campaign against Abercrombie & Fitch unless they promised not to use Australian wool. PETA reportedly sent copies of sample critical advertisements they intended to use which had catch-phrases such as "Ditch the Fitch" and "Abercrombie or Abercruelty." Abercrombie & Fitch yielded to the threat, confirming in writing to PETA that it would not buy Australian wool.

PETA's concern was that Australian wool-growing practices were inhumane, in particular the practice of "mulesing" which requires the cutting of the backside of the sheep to prevent the sheep from becoming flyblown. A PETA spokesperson said that of the two dozen or so other clothing retailers to which they had issued demands, some had responded and some hadn't, and so PETA was in the process of deciding which retailer(s) it would proceed to target.

Australian wool growers responded in a press release on October 15, 2004, advising that Abercrombie & Fitch did not even use Australian wool. The press release continued that Australia was the world's largest and most advanced wool producer, that PETA was a radical group that even opposed recreational fishing, that the Royal Society for the Prevention of Cruelty to Animals (RSPCA) accepted mulesing as a necessary practice and that without mulesing, for which alternative procedures were being researched (an effort to which PETA was not contributing or funding), sheep would die painfully from becoming flyblown.

*(continued)*

*(continued)*

PETA's Website on October 18, 2004, trumped the other players in this drama by advising that PETA had announced "an Australian wool boycott with American retailer Abercrombie & Fitch at its side" and presenting as its new partner and champion, Abercrombie & Fitch, which had "set a new standard" by joining the boycott.

Sources: *The Weekend Australian* newspaper, October 15, 2004, p. 8; a joint release from Australian Wool Innovation and the Australian National Farmers' Federation, October 15, 2004; and www.peta.org, October 18, 2004.

of civil society, are producing a form of endogenous change within multinational corporations. Like many of the international development agencies, NGOs are also moving away from encouraging limitations on corporate involvement in development and instead are demanding that MNCs do more. Oxfam International, for example, has asked the world's business community to support an end to agricultural production and export subsidies in the European Union and the United States, and many MNCs are buying into this as witnessed at the biennial Congress of the International Chamber of Commerce in Marrakech in June 2004.[15]

## NGOs as Watchdogs and Monitors

As we have noted, NGOs do much more than attack corporations; they are also watchdogs, monitors, and collaborators. In addition, they are involved in advocacy and lobbying work, humanitarian relief, and social work. Under contract with governmental aid agencies such as the United States Agency for International Development (USAID), they have become key implementers of direct international development assistance to people in developing countries, delivering food, medicine, and humanitarian relief of all sorts.[16] (Forty percent of the budgets of NGOs come from governments.) But they are also involved well beyond the basic development agenda. They have lobbied to create the international ban on land mines and for the formation of the International

Criminal Court, and have had a powerful impact on the agendas of a host of international organizations such as the International Monetary Fund, the World Trade Organization, the United Nations Environment Fund, the United Nations Development Programme, and the World Bank. Half the World Bank's lending projects provide for NGO involvement in some form or other.

Nowadays, governments and especially international development agencies refuse to take the lead on many projects without the backing of relevant NGOs. "Participatory dialogue," "stakeholder consultation," and "inclusive engagement" are all requirements for policy and project development. The heads of intergovernmental agencies feel uncomfortably exposed unless they are cloaked with some form of imprimatur from the nebulous "civil society."

This trend is not without critics.[17] The fact that NGOs can influence the decisions of intergovernmental agencies such as the World Bank, especially if the Bank is dealing with a democratically elected government, does not sit well with some. As one author noted, "Many borrowing governments complain that it is inappropriate for the World Bank to anoint non-elected, self-styled representatives of civil society to interfere."[18] Former U.S. Secretary of Treasury and World Bank chief economist Lawrence Summers said, "I am deeply troubled by the distance the Bank has gone in democratic countries toward engagement with groups other than governments in designing projects."[19] But Summers conceded that "if you are a development organization, you really cannot be in bad grace with the principal carriers of moral energy around development."[20] This is an assessment that many have come to learn and even accept as a result of scarring experiences. Of course, the better NGOs earn their place at the table. They often have excellent staff, many of whom rotate throughout their careers between formal institutions and civil society organizations. But decision-makers in the United Nations and its agencies and the World Bank remain uncertain about the optimal extent of NGO involvement.

In fact, new terms have arisen to describe the role NGOs are playing in setting policies, agendas, and parameters for acceptable behavior: terms such as "soft law" and "civil regulation" describe this role. This is why governments and intergovernmental organizations as well as MNC managers increasingly feel that the lack of a civil society imprimatur amounts to an absence of legitimacy, even where there is no formal or legal requirement for NGO involvement. Nowadays, major new resource projects begin and end as often with social impact assessments by NGOs as with engineering studies or cost-benefit analyses. BP's early-stage interaction with NGOs and development agencies in connection with its massive Tangguh project in Indonesia is a case in point, although by no means the exception these days, especially in the wounded extractive industries. See box 3.3 for some background.

Although NGOs see themselves at the forefront of the fight against poverty, their criticism of development agencies such as the World Bank may not help the poor at all. *Washington Post* columnist Sebastion Mallaby concluded in a review of NGO opposition to World Bank funding of dams in poor countries that the war against poverty is threatened by friendly fire. "A swarm of media-savvy Western activists has descended upon aid agencies, staging protests to block projects that allegedly exploit the developing world. The protests serve professional agitators by keeping their pet causes in the headlines. But they do not always serve the millions of people who live without clean water or electricity."[21]

Among the NGOs most active in "countering" the activities of MNCs is the U.S.-based CorpWatch.[22] It claims to have led the exposure of the deplorable working conditions in the Vietnamese apparel factories that supplied Nike in the mid-1990s. It also played a leading role in opposing the UN's plan to collaborate more closely with large corporations in 1998 (see box 5.7 in chapter 5, which explains the failed Global Sustainable Development Facility proposal). A CorpWatch news release of June 2000 regarding this achievement stated: "The criticisms of the GSDF included associating with corporate bad actors, an overemphasis on the free-market ideology of globalization and development, the danger of 'bluewash' by corporations hoping for public relations benefits from wrapping themselves in the flag of the United Nations, and failure to abide by the agency's own guidelines in associating with private companies."[23] CorpWatch advised that "even with the end of the GSDF, we will remain vigilant in tracking other UN-corporate partnership programs."[24]

Box 3.3

### BP's Tangguh Project in Papua, Indonesia

BP is developing one of the world's largest new gas fields. It is located not far off the northwest coast of the remote Indonesian province of Berau Bintuni in the eastern region of Papua. The resource was discovered in the mid-1990s and originally tapped in 1997. It is broken into three separate fields. BP is the project operator and currently owns 37 percent of the project. As a new project, BP's executives wanted to get things right from the outset. But to BP's current management, that meant not just ensuring correct engineering and geology reports as well as environmental impact assessments, but also conducting major social and economic impact assessments and designing development projects in response.

Recognizing that they lacked both the experience and the legitimacy to conduct this sort of undertaking themselves, BP contracted the UK and U.S. development agencies, the Department for International Development (DFID) and the U.S. Agency for International Development (USAID) respectively, to carry out the required work. Experts from the World Bank and others such as the consulting firm Ernst and Young have also assisted. Reports and actions plans have also been prepared regarding human resettlement issues, human rights provisions, and environmental safeguards. Various specialist development NGOs were recruited to assist. All of this has been built into an Integrated Social Strategy (ISS) and has been made subject to monitoring by a standing Tangguh Independent Advisory Panel (TIAP). The strategy includes, for example, training and education programs, health care facilities, local economic development initiatives, and environmental and heritage protection measures. The UNDP is involved with its "Capacity 2015" project called "Partnerships for Sustainable Development in Papua, Indonesia."

*(continued)*

*(continued)*

As part of this ongoing process, BP will be leading a series of meetings and workshops, not just in Papua or Jakarta, but in global capitals, with NGOs, socially responsible investors, development agencies, and other interested parties. It is interesting to note that the ISS includes a range of social, economic, and environmental performance indicators and appears much like the framework of a development project being implemented by a development agency rather than an old-style business plan.

SOURCES: www.bp.com, USAID documentation, and involved practitioners.

NGOs like CorpWatch, notwithstanding their small budgets and staff, are seemingly able to garner large audiences for their views and rapidly organize criticism of MNC activity, whether wrongdoing is proven or not. They somehow have a powerful license to act as a watchdog without any formal mandate or recourse to a particular legal framework. CorpWatch is not alone. Numerous NGOs are entirely devoted to monitoring MNC behavior, although their objectives vary widely, leaving MNC managers, who might be quite willing to respond positively to a reasonable NGO request, often uncertain about what is expected of them.

Sometimes it does not even take an NGO to have a profound impact on an MNC. Made with a small budget and watched the world over, the 2004 documentary movie, *Super Size Me*, which showed the dietary risks faced by consumers who regularly frequented the fast-food restaurants of the global chain McDonald's, pushed the company into a series of changes to its operations and products. Another example is the 2004 Canadian documentary movie *The Corporation*, which traces the legal and historical underpinnings of the corporation to dramatize its power today. (Box 3.4 provides a snapshot of the movie.) The directors wrote: "One hundred and fifty years ago the corporation was a relatively insignificant entity. Today it is a vivid, dramatic and pervasive presence in all our lives. Like the Church, the Monarchy and the Communist Party in other times and places, the corporation is today's dominant institu-

## Box 3.4

### *The Corporation*—A Documentary Movie

*The Corporation* uses a series of interviews and case studies to analyze a generic corporation. After detailing the historical reasons
behind the Anglo-Saxon legal system's definition of a corporation
as an individual entity, or a "legal person," the film goes on to
conclude that when compared against World Health Organization criteria, a corporation is, in fact, psychopathic. "It is self-
interested, inherently amoral, callous, and deceitful; it breaches
social and legal standards to get its way; it does not suffer from
guilt, yet it can mimic the human qualities of empathy, caring,
and altruism." In short, the movie argues that the corporation has
all the rights of individuals, is infinitely more powerful than individuals, but, lacking the normal behavioral instincts of a healthy
individual, it is dangerous and destructive.

The movie examines pressures on corporate activities such as
the drive for eco-efficiency, increasing calls for corporations to be
more sustainable, and even for non-owners of corporate capital to
have a say in corporate activities. It touches on efforts by Interface,
the world's largest carpet maker, to improve its eco-efficiency, as
well as the problems faced by Shell in Nigeria and elsewhere. The
film interviewed thinkers like Noam Chomsky, Milton Friedman,
and Peter Drucker; social critics like Michael Moore; and corporate leaders like Shell's Sir Mark Moody-Stuart. It addressed the
question of whether corporate staff members are individually responsible for overall corporate behavior (and generally agrees that
they are) and considers the problems that beset whistle-blowers.

*(continued)*

tion. But history humbles dominant institutions. All have been crushed,
belittled or absorbed into some new order. The corporation is unlikely
to be the first to defy history."[25]

In explaining the motivation behind the movie, one of the filmmakers wrote: "The problem was especially pressing because, with economic

*(continued)*

The movie argues that major corporations often undermine democracy by dealing with undemocratic regimes, influencing legislative processes unduly, or trying to overthrow properly elected governments. The filmmakers conclude that individuals and communities are fighting back and that "as global individuals take back local power, a growing re-invigoration of the concept of citizenship is taking root. It has the power to not only strip the corporation of its seeming omnipotence, but to create a feeling and an ideology of democracy that is much more than its mere institutional version."

SOURCE: www.thecorporation.com.

globalization in full swing, corporations were emerging as global governing institutions, dominating societies and governments throughout the world. At the same time, most people had, and have, very little understanding of their true institutional nature. So it made sense to ask: What is the nature of this new governing institution? And what are the consequences of its growing hold on society? . . . (The idea developed) that the corporation, deemed by the law to be a person, had a psychopathic personality and that there was something quite bizarre, and dangerous, in such an institution wielding so much power."

## Collaborators

Although some NGOs consider MNCs and the globalization they drive to be inherently bad, others pursue their objectives in cooperation with companies. The Center for Global Development, for example, focuses on the effectiveness of international aid and the reduction of poverty in developing countries. Based in Washington, D.C., CGD studies issues related to globalization, economic policies to help the poor, and the steps required for necessary policy reforms.

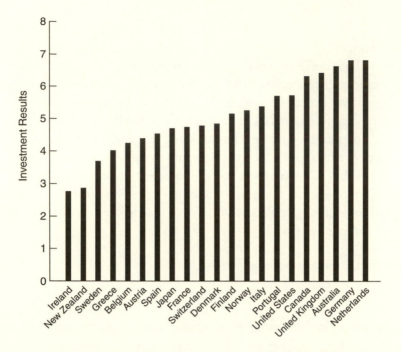

Figure 3.1. CGD 2004 Commitment to Development Index—Investment
Component. Source: Center for Global Development and Foreign Policy
Commitment to Development Index 2004.

Among other things, CGD is concerned with the role international
investment by large MNCs plays in providing a more equitable spread
of global opportunity and wealth. As part of its efforts to monitor the
factors that affect poverty reduction in developing countries, CGD has
developed an index for measuring and ranking the performance and
commitment of a set of rich countries with respect to global development
and poverty reduction. Although this Commitment to Development
Index is understandably controversial, it nevertheless provides a benchmark that was not previously available. CGD's CDI assesses twenty-
one rich countries against a large number of factors bundled into seven
components, one of which deals with developed countries' promotion
and facilitation of investment in developing countries (see figure 3.1).

This is an important recognition of the role of foreign investment
in development and poverty reduction and the part developed country
governments can play in encouraging their own major companies to

invest in poor countries. (We address this topic further, together with the issue of "home country incentives," in chapter 7.) In determining the rankings of the twenty-one rich countries by the "investment" criterion, CGD looked at a number of factors, including, for example, whether the home government provides political risk insurance for companies operating abroad and whether provisions to prevent double taxation are in place. (Box 3.5 further details the factors taken into account for the investment component of the CDI.)

An example of a different kind of cooperative interaction between NGOs and multinational corporations is Transparency International's advocacy of the 1997 OECD Bribery Convention (see box 3.6).

## Local Partnerships

Large numbers of smaller NGOs or local branches of international NGOs work at the country level with MNCs in developing countries. Multinational corporations report that they find these sorts of local NGO partnerships easier to enter, more likely to produce results, and less subject to vacuous posturing than collaboration with large, global NGOs. Said Gerard Mastrelatt, CEO of the giant French energy company, Suez: "On the ground, NGOs are capable of helping us to get in touch with the local inhabitants and play the role of mediator. A large company can often engender a feeling of distrust, even if our intentions are good. The NGO can help create a climate of trust between the local people and the company."[26]

As these sorts of working-level partnerships between MNCs and NGOs become more commonplace, there is growing evidence of a convergence of objectives between these two vastly different forms of organization. MNCs are taking more notice of social objectives, NGOs are becoming more business-oriented (as illustrated in figure 3.2). This convergence is being brought about over time by, on one side, the increasing commercialization of NGO-type organizations, which are adopting business-type practices and seeking revenue streams and profit sources to help ensure their sustainability and effectiveness and, on the other side, the adoption by companies of multiple social and community objectives, which are viewed as a way of accruing legitimacy and under-

## Box 3.5

### CGD's CDI Index and Considerations
### for Investment Flows

The CDI index's investment component assessed the twenty-one
rich countries' performance against five main factors.

(i) *The provision of political risk insurance.* Considers
whether the country is a member of a multilateral
political risk insurance system and whether it has its
own national insurance provider. Also takes into account whether the insurer examines the economic impact of the project in the recipient country if, for example, the investment is subsidized or somehow
creates distortions.

(ii) *Preventive arrangements for double taxation.* Considers
whether double taxation agreements are in place, then
examines the characteristics and extent of those
agreements if, for example, there are tax-sparing
provisions and if host economy tax concessions are
permitted. Also values, at a lesser level, the existence of bilateral investment treaties.

(iii) *Adoption of national or international anticorruption
covenants.* Considers accession to the OECD's
bribery convention and whether there is monitoring
under that convention. Also considers whether
there is participation in "publish-what-you-pay"-type
initiatives and the country's score on Transparency
International's Bribe Payers' Index.

(iv) *Other foreign direct investment facilitation measures.*
Considers the accessibility of dispute resolution mechanisms, support to developing country investment promotion agencies, and facilitative support for outward investment to developing countries.

*(continued)*

*(continued)*

(v) *Promotion of inward portfolio investment.* Considers whether technical assistance is on offer to support the securities industry and capital markets in developing countries and whether investment funds are restricted or prevented from investing in developing countries.

SOURCE: Drawn from Theodore H. Moran's paper: "Rationale for Components of a Scoring System of Developed Country Support for International Investment Flows to Developing Countries," March 9, 2004, working paper; available online at www.cgdev.org/rankingtherich/docs/investment_2004.pdf.

pinning their mainstream activities. Philip Watts, former chairman of the Committee of Managing Directors of the Royal Dutch/Shell Group, pointed to this convergence when he wrote: "The need to balance economic, social, and environmental considerations makes it a very powerful concept. It provides common ground for discussion. Businesses sometimes think only about economic considerations. NGOs sometimes think only about the environment, or only about social issues. Sustainable development forces us all to confront the reality of integrating those considerations and making hard choices."[27] This sentiment was echoed in June 2004 by Farouk Jiwa, director of Honey Care Africa, a community-based social organization in Kenya (see box 5.3 later in the book for details); "Trust me," Jiwa remarked, "businesses and NGOs are getting closer, becoming more alike, all the time."

An interesting manifestation of this is the changes that have occurred in corporate mission statements over time. These are a useful reflection of how companies view themselves and what they do. A brief review of early mission statements reveals that before World War II they were generally along the lines of: "Our function is to make widgets and sell them profitably." Starting in the 1950s, at least in the United States, these mission statements gradually but steadily changed.[28] In general, they began to add to an explanation of the core business other assorted functions such as: "to look after our staff"; "to satisfy our customers"; "to consider the environment"; "to work closely with suppliers, partners,

## Box 3.6

### Transparency International and
### the OECD Bribery Convention

For many years U.S. multinational corporations unsuccessfully lobbied successive U.S. administrations to repeal the United States' Foreign Corrupt Practices Act. Large U.S. companies felt that other foreign multinational corporations, not bound by the same anticorruption impositions of this Act, were out-competing the U.S. companies in securing contracts and business deals around the world, especially in developing countries. When lobbying efforts targeted at the U.S. government failed at home, these U.S. companies sought to level the international corporate playing field in another way. They moved to have the international rules of business changed to outlaw bribery. The forum of the OECD was the chosen mechanism for this, with the OECD Bribery Convention ultimately imposing on companies registered in OECD member countries binding requirements not to adopt corrupt practices.

In parallel with a concerted push by the U.S. State Department, U.S. MNCs solicited the support of Transparency International to lobby OECD member governments and OECD delegates to adopt the Bribery Convention. There was considerable initial resistance to the initiative, especially from some European countries, but the political lobbying work conducted by Transparency International and some other NGOs, strongly encouraged by various U.S. MNCs, eventually succeeded in making corrupt payments in overseas business practices unlawful in OECD home jurisdictions.

SOURCES: P. J. Simmons, "Learning to Live with NGOs," *Foreign Policy* 112 (Fall 1998), p. 86, and former OECD and Transparency International staff.

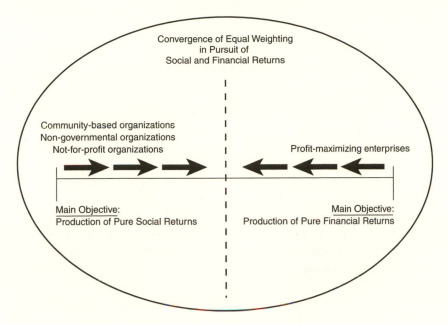

Figure 3.2. Continuing convergence of objectives of corporations and NGOs.

neighbors, and other stakeholders"; then later adding "to lessen adverse social impacts"; and more recently "to produce social benefits." Increasingly, corporations around the world are partnering with NGOs to define what those benefits are and how they are to be achieved.

MNCs are also increasingly using local NGOs as part of their business platform. For example, Procter & Gamble, a U.S. multinational producer of personal cleaning and hygiene goods, has trained and assisted a local NGO in Haiti to distribute and market an inexpensive additive to make potable drinking water (see box 3.7 for details).

There exist a growing number of examples of businesses seeking local partnership arrangements rather than global umbrella agreements with larger international NGOs. One consequence of NGO-business partnerships such as these is that multinational corporations come to regard the details and mechanics of the approaches they take to local NGO partnerships, just like their regular supply-chain arrangements and distribution networks, as matters to be held in confidence. MNCs are thus unlikely to publicize the reasons when such a partner-

## Box 3.7

### Procter & Gamble and a Haitian NGO

In 2004 Procter & Gamble won a World Business Award that was jointly presented by the International Chamber of Commerce, the International Business Leaders Forum, and the United Nations Development Programme. The award was offered in support of the United Nations Millennium Development Goals. One of four winners, P & G won for research and development related to production of a low-cost additive to make potable drinking water.

P & G has developed a water treatment system in partnership with the International Council of Nurses (ICN) and the U.S. Centers for Disease Control and Prevention (CDC). After more than ten years in development, the company is still working to bring the product to market. It will cost about one cent per liter to produce treated, drinkable water and so even the poorest should be able to take advantage of the product. It is intended to be sold in sachet form. It will be particularly useful where flows of regular water have been cut, for example, after natural disasters or war. But proving the product, "PuR Purifier of Water," in the market is expensive and difficult. P & G has already conducted trials in several developing countries including Pakistan, Guatemala, Morocco, Botswana, Liberia, and the Philippines.

Sustainable and profitable distribution of the product was identified as a challenge because of the low margins involved. P & G selected Haiti to conduct a trial for low-cost distribution that would ensure efficient delivery to key users of the product, that is, the poorest people in remote places. In a trial in Haiti P & G decided to partner with a local NGO. This initially involved providing extensive training and new resources to the NGO. The upside for P & G was limited direct country risk, low investment, and strengthened local distribution and country knowledge. The approach of partnering with a local rather than international NGO proved particularly effective, mainly because it was close to the ground and better informed about market and distribution issues.

Sources: International Chamber of Commerce 2004 World Business Awards Presentation and Procter & Gamble.

ship with a local NGO succeeds. This is understandable but regrettable because it slows the timely replication of best practice arrangements for business partnerships between MNCs and NGOs in developing countries.

There are many other examples of NGOs collaborating with MNCs. One involves the Global Reporting Initiative, an independent agency loosely connected to the United Nations and referred to as a "collaborating center of the United Nations Environment Programme."[29] GRI encourages MNCs to report their activities and corporate social responsibility programs, especially those that focus on sustainable development, and to invest more in monitoring activities to measure environmental, social, and economic values and impacts. It designs and promotes voluntary guidelines that facilitate companies' adoption of a uniform reporting framework for the economic, social, and environmental impacts of activities, products, and services. GRI calls this "sustainability reporting." In essence, the organization is trying to replicate in the social field the greater harmonization in corporate financial reporting that has occurred in recent decades. It hopes to make possible the comparison of results and performance over time, across countries, and among industry sectors.

In October 2004 a large group of investment firms (representing $147 billion in funds under management) called on companies to adopt GRI's reporting principles. The investment firms encouraged this for two reasons. First, they increasingly want to value the nonfinancial performance of companies in which they invest or in which they wish to invest. Second, it helps them compare apples with apples. "Companies have been asking us for guidance on how to meet the skyrocketing demands for information," said Steve Lippmann, senior social research analyst for Trillium Asset Management. "With this statement, we recommend ways that companies can increase the credibility, comparability, and utility of their reporting." "Our stakeholders look to us to disclose key environmental and social data so they can compare and judge our performance," said Dave Stangis, director of corporate responsibility for Intel. "It makes clear sense for Intel to meet that need."[30]

Another example is the Center for International Private Enterprise (CIPE), an arm of the U.S. National Endowment for Democracy affiliated with the U.S. Chamber of Commerce that focuses on the development of the private sector and on strengthening the institutions that underpin private-sector growth and promote democracy. CIPE makes grants to developing-country business associations, local NGOs, and academic institutes that focus on legislative advocacy, promotion of economic reform, and economic policy training for local decision-makers. Organizations such as CIPE, which can hardly be described as radical, seem to have been able to fill a gap in project implementation options that elude many NGOs and development consulting firms.

Some NGOs develop close links to business to help achieve their aims. One such organization is the Prince of Wales International Business Leaders Forum (IBLF) of the United Kingdom. Unlike other organizations that focus on corporate social responsibility, IBLF is not a representative body. It does not implement projects or undertake partnership projects with MNCs. Its priority tasks are advocacy and dissemination of best practice models. Originally focused strictly on corporate social responsibility as that was broadly understood in the early 1990s, it has evolved to take into account the full range of opportunities for business to play a constructive role in development. In addition to a continuing focus on CSR, it makes a case for business to advance and spread the social benefits that its activities can bring about. As an example of its activities, in May 2005 it held a symposium entitled, "Business and Development: Business Models for Meeting Development Challenges," which addressed the issue of engaging more with business in the fight against global poverty.

Other NGOs serve more of a coordinating function. The World Association of Investment Promotion Agencies (WAIPA), a Swiss-based NGO, recruits as members country and territory investment promotion organizations from around the world. Established with the help of the United Nations Conference on Trade and Development (UNCTAD), WAIPA's main task is to help its members become more competent at attracting foreign investment to their home economies. It disseminates best practice, conducts training, and convenes exchanges on policy and operational options. The key target market for most IPAs is inward investment by major multinational corporations or their subsidiaries and affiliates. WAIPA also brings to its meetings representatives of MNCs who offer to government officials responsible for attracting inward investment their own insights into MNC requirements. Often in conjunction with UNCTAD (see chapter 5), WAIPA seeks to fashion mechanisms for enhancing linkages between MNCs and host economy businesses.

Some NGOs resemble businesses in the way they operate. Business for Social Responsibility (BSR), for example, a U.S.-based organization formed in 1992 that helps member companies "achieve success in ways that respect ethical values, people, communities and the environment,"[31] was established by a small group of U.S. firms seeking to be simultaneously "commercially successful and socially responsible."[32] It is a prime example of an NGO/consulting organization, a number of which have moved into the field of helping firms, often large multinational firms, improve their social responsibility activities. Although incorporated as a not-for-profit organization, it seeks fee-based consulting assignments from businesses in the manner of commercial consulting firms. (For-profit firms are also moving into the field, Delta Pearl of the UK being one example.) BSR adds to the literature on CSR through regular publications and the use of a strong network of business groups and international organizations. It partners with like-minded NGOs such as CSR Europe, based in Brussels, and Japan's Council for Better Corporate Citizenship. BSR was also a co-contributor to the "how-to" book for the UN's Global Compact, *Raising the Bar: Creating Value with the UN's Global Compact*.

NGOs are now working much more closely with businesses toward which they were once perceived to be antagonistic. The World Resources Institute (WRI), established more than twenty years ago, has, like many other NGOs that formerly focused primarily on environmental issues, adopted a broader mandate that takes into account issues such as equitable development and sustainability. In 2004, WRI hosted a large conference that emphasized "bottom of the pyramid" thinking about how to alleviate poverty in developing countries;[33] that is, an emphasis on encouraging corporations to focus more on the mass poor of the world and delivering better and cheaper services to that market. The broadening of WRI's focus is further evidence of the growing international consensus concerning poverty reduction and the growing number of diverse organizations that are linking their missions to it.

## Conclusion

NGOs in all their variety appear, much as Teilhard de Chardin foresaw, to reflect a rising global consciousness, perhaps even a conscience, advancing with no particular mandate in communities in which government is inadequate for the task and in which the forces of globalization have inadequately defined and promoted community needs. The NGOs have proven highly effective in using the media and various forums to promote their point of view. And large corporations have come to fear and sometimes to respect them. Although often dismissed as public relations exercises or a "greenwash," MNCs' conciliatory responses to the calls of the NGOs are ever so gradually being seen as not only legitimate, but even genuine and useful. This positive trend is likely to accelerate as the interests, objectives, and scope of activities of MNCs and NGOs continue to converge.

It is clear that NGOs, like MNCs, are here to stay. Both are increasingly interested in reducing poverty, and in a growing number of instances NGOs have helped MNCs improve their effectiveness in achieving these objectives. But there is much more that NGOs could do to help corporations bring their capabilities to bear on the problems of the poor; indeed, it is unlikely that NGOs concerned with poverty reduction can succeed without MNCs.

In chapter 4 we examine the corporate response to the NGO attack and in chapter 6 consider the extent to which the international governmental and intergovernmental development agencies make use of MNCs to drive sustainable, positive, poverty-reducing change. Let us conclude here by saying that there is no way to produce such change unless the three sets of players—NGOs, MNCs, and governmental agencies—work more closely together.

# 4

# The Corporate Response

Pressed by NGOs and leaders in the international community such as the secretary-general of the United Nations to contribute more effectively to social improvements, multinational corporations have undertaken a wide variety of initiatives in response. Some MNCs have made wholesale changes in the way they operate, some even in what they do. In response to these myriad and changing pressures, sometimes confounded business leaders have gone back to first principles. They have asked themselves what it is that they actually stand for and what is expected of them. Used to taking instructions from investors and government, they find now that everyone wants to direct them. Business leaders are increasingly giving voice to this uncertainty and pressure for change. As Lord Browne, chairman of BP, recently rhetorically asked: "What is the role of business? What do people expect of companies, especially large, global corporations? Where can we contribute to human progress? What is our capability and our legitimacy?"[1]

He isn't alone in asking these questions, or in attempting to respond in a surefooted and constructive manner. And, as we have seen, companies are increasingly inclined to respond, albeit somewhat haphazardly. The creaky response reflects neither recalcitrance nor intransigence; these enterprises often are simply uncertain. Many business leaders are now starting to ask the same questions as Lord Browne, but the answers remain elusive.

Corporate responses fall under several headings: corporate social responsibility; industry codes of conduct; accession to various agreed sets of behavioral principles; collaboration with the United Nations and other intergovernmental agencies; sustainable development initiatives; and the formation of innumerable international councils and committees. None as yet has made a substantial impact on global poverty, but we review them here to help us understand the inadequacy of the corporate response to the growing demands that business be more mindful of its impact on and responsibility for the communities that it affects.

Corporations large and small have long been aware of their "social responsibility," notwithstanding considerable disagreement about the meaning of the term and its various versions and implications. Milton Friedman, as we mentioned earlier, made one side of the argument famous more than forty years ago when he vehemently denied any responsibility beyond obeying the law:

> Few trends could so thoroughly undermine the very foundations of our society as the acceptance by corporate officials of a social responsibility other than to make as much money for the stockholders as possible. This is a fundamentally subversive doctrine. If businessmen do have a social responsibility other than making maximum profits for stockholders, how are they to know what it is? Can self-selected private individuals decide what the social interest is?[2]

Friedman's answer was "no." Only government can determine that interest. What Friedman seems to have ignored is that many governments are not regarded as reliable definers or implementers of "the social interest." So as a practical matter, corporate managers have for a number of reasons—image, employee satisfaction, general acceptability—felt obliged to go beyond profit and contribute to the communities they affect in some larger way. Impact on shareholder value might be hard to measure, but a survey of one thousand companies in Canada in 2000 found that corporate social activities contributed to enhanced reputation.[3] The IFC has also found that MNC investment in sustainable environmental initiatives, socially directed investments, and improved corporate governance generally have a positive if hard-to-measure effect on the corporate bottomline.[4]

## Corporate Social Responsibility

In recent years this sense of obligation has exploded into what some see as a "radical reinterpretation of the role of private business, a new model for capitalism."[5] It is the Corporate Social Responsibility movement with a capital "C", "S," and "R." The most recent definition of CSR, as adopted by the World Bank, is: "The commitment of business to contribute to sustainable economic development working with employees, their families, the local community and society at large to improve their quality of life, in ways that are both good for business and good for development."[6]

The CSR movement has undoubtedly produced some good results. It has prodded multinational corporations to adopt safer, healthier, more environmentally friendly practices and to work to achieve more equitable distribution of the benefits derived from their activities. It is also, however, attracting a band of critics. CSR, they say, is the product of "wooly thinking" by the enemies of "capitalism." They assert that the time is coming when a perfectly legitimate business could be unfairly deprived of its "license to operate" because it does not have an "acceptable" CSR program in place.[7]

CSR and all its meanings have changed much over time and different views and expectations of it abound. At an August 2004 seminar convened by the World Bank Institute, CSR was exuberantly described as "a crucial element of international efforts to foster sustainable and equitable development worldwide." A representative of a Chilean NGO involved in presenting the seminar observed that "interest in CSR has increased greatly in recent years across the Americas and has sparked some innovative approaches linking CSR with national competitiveness and development."[8] So now CSR, far from being a representation of old-style "corporate citizenship," is being fashioned as a tool for development as well as for gaining competitive economic advantage in the developing world.

Its critics, however, charge that CSR sometimes does more harm than good: efficient corporate producers of goods or services that are socially beneficial are required to invest in extraneous CSR-related activities instead of getting better at and focusing more on their core function. The critics argue that the distraction of CSR might reduce efficiency and the ability to innovate, all leading to a net loss to society.

Large corporations that operate internationally are increasingly reporting that outside pressure for CSR is having a profound effect on their investment decisions. They often will not make new investments in a developing country or forge a link to local suppliers if there are doubts about the prevailing CSR framework.[9] That is, if the mother company finds an inadequate CSR framework in a poor country, it will often choose not to invest there because of risk to the overall global brand reputation. Thus, in this context the Chilean NGO representative might be right: being better at CSR might bring advantages to one developing country over another. Others will say that the requirement for CSR is now being foisted by rich countries on the poor ones and this represents yet another cost of production that they can little afford in a tightly competitive global market. Some will say it is the introduction of yet another barrier to export from poor countries to the rich world.

If CSR or something like it is here to stay, and we believe it is, the question then becomes how to manage it so that it is both efficient for business and effective for the community. We shall briefly examine some of the CSR-related responses below.


## Industry Standards and Codes of Conduct

Bertrand Collomb, chairman of Lafarge, the French construction company, argued that "business faces growing pressure from society to help ensure that the benefits of this newly globalized world are distributed equitably."[10] "Many multinational companies," he added, "are moving beyond conventional wisdom and working with new partners as engines of national development, helping communities lift themselves out of poverty and into market economies."[11] Examples include the chemical industry's adoption of safety standards in the wake of the disaster in Bhopal, India, and the Montreal Protocol to reduce or eliminate the production of chlorofluorocarbons that destroy the earth's ozone layer. Mining companies often cultivate relationships with local NGOs in order to help assure governments that their activities are safe and healthy.

Global corporations are also establishing a variety of so-called "certification" arrangements—codes of conduct, production guidelines, and monitoring standards that govern their behavior and that of their suppliers around the world. In 2001 the OECD listed 246 codes of conduct in existence, and many more have been added since. One of the more well-known standards for a code of conduct for MNCs is SA8000. Some background details are contained in box 4.1.

---

Box 4.1

### SA8000

SA8000 was created and managed by Social Accountability International, a U.S.-based not-for-profit organization that aims to develop, monitor, and verify voluntary social accountability standards. It commenced development of SA8000 in 1996. Described by SAI as a "way for retailers, brand companies, suppliers and other organizations to maintain just and decent working conditions throughout the supply chain," it has since become widely accepted. Largely focused on labor conditions and the rights of workers, SA8000 is closely aligned with the ILO's basic conditions for workers and the UN's human rights conventions and declarations. It includes provisions related to forced labor, health and safety, working conditions, rights to collective association, and workplace discrimination and provides for factory-level management systems and compliance verification and monitoring systems.

SOURCE: Social Accountability International.

---

Standards such as these are becoming so pervasive and accepted that, though voluntary, they are verging on becoming a form of law. When implemented by an international operator in a foreign country they might, in some respects, replace the local law. "In contrast to the classic terrain of legal pluralist analysis, . . . law developed by corporations to govern their own relationships—these corporate self-regulatory initiatives—enable (multinational corporations) to extend their laws directly to workers along the global production chain, disregarding, even undermining, local enforcement efforts."[12] This risk is especially apparent in developing countries. Where governmental institutions are weak, these imported conventions and codes might obscure or erode the role of local government. This is especially troubling when it affects government regulation of MNCs.[13]

MNC managers are, of course, fully aware of this dichotomy, but the means to escape it is not always obvious. They know that in upholding international standards that are often drafted by rich world NGOs they might well be undermining local traditions, for example, the appropriate age at which a child should work or the relative importance of an endangered species or forest. Not by design but by default the MNC finds itself in some ways its own regulator, behaving as if it were a local government.

Standards and codes abound in both number and variety. One of the first codes of its kind, the Sullivan Principles developed by the Reverend Leon Sullivan in the United States in 1978 to address primarily labor conditions and workers' rights, was eventually incorporated into the U.S. 1986 Comprehensive Anti-Apartheid Act, with binding effect for U.S. companies operating in South Africa, forcing change from prevailing practices. A newer industry code, the Equator Principles, led by the International Finance Corporation and adopted in 2003 by ten global banks, includes standards relating to the environment, social issues, human rights, and the heritage of indigenous communities, to which the banks agreed to adhere when making project loans. By 2004, eighteen more banks had signed on. Given the power of these banks one might suppose that adoption of the principles would have an important effect, and that may well prove to be the case, but a recent study by three Duke University professors found such codes in the past to be "blunt and imperfect tools." They noted the fear that "certification driven by activists and corporations will preempt or supplant altogether the role of states and international organizations in addressing corporate accountability." There is the additional fear that the various codes of conduct and their monitoring agencies will undermine the role of unions in developing countries.[14]

There has been much arguing over codes, auditing, and implementation with some companies proceeding on their own and others seeking a collective approach. Some apparel companies, for example, are now themselves co-funding, along with USAID, the development of corporate codes of conduct for garment producers and distributors in Central America (see box 4.2 for details). Germany's Federal Ministry for Economic Cooperation and Development has launched several similar initiatives as part of its "Public-Private Partnership Programme." The German authorities promoted discussion among private-sector operators, trade unions, and civil society groups that led to the adoption of a

---

Box 4.2

### USAID, DAI, and Multinational
### Apparel Companies in Guatemala

Multinational apparel firms, both manufacturers and buyers, are these days acutely aware of the risks their brand reputations face should they be charged with exploiting labor in poor countries. Their touchstone is the threat that was posed to the Nike brand following accusations of poor labor practices in garment factories in Vietnam in the 1990s. A handful of apparel companies have, therefore, gladly agreed to cofinance with USAID a program in Guatemala to establish approved standards of labor conditions in apparel factories in that country. With the legitimacy and impartiality of the process paramount, the companies are co-funding a leading independent development consulting firm, Development Alternatives Inc. (DAI), to manage the process in partnership with USAID. The project will develop consistent voluntary codes of compliance among local manufacturers and distributors. This is an important way of improving standards along global supply chains and helps foreign buyers ensure higher and more consistent standards among their developing country suppliers.

SOURCE: DAI's Global Business Solutions Practice, 2004.

---

code of conduct for trade in garments covering some 15 developing countries and 1,600 suppliers. In conjunction with fair trade groups, coffee buyers and producers, and NGOs, the German government also established a code of conduct for sustainable coffee production.[15]

Some progress has been reported in the working conditions prevailing in the apparel factories in developing countries, but the sad truth is that the impact of the campaign on poverty in the developing world has been slight. Even if wages and working conditions improve significantly, apparel represents only 14 percent of total exports and a mere 3 percent of the GDP of low-income countries.[16] If poverty reduction is the goal, then something more, much more, is required. Of course, we can deduce that the goal of NGOs working in this particular field is not poverty reduction but promotion of improved working conditions. Some companies, in fact, acknowledge their reluctance to invest in developing countries owing to the risk that they might be exposed to charges of human rights violations among the poor in their local work force.

Partially in response to such reports, the International Organization for Standardization recently decided to develop an international standard for social responsibility (see box 4.3). The ISO is best known for its myriad technical standards, ISO 9000 and ISO 14000 being two prominent examples. These standards broadly deal with production quality management and environmental management, respectively. But in a significant shift, senior ISO officials meeting in Sweden in June 2004 agreed that there was a role for ISO to play in setting standards for the social responsibilities of big business. This is a further example of how crowded this field is becoming, and how popular. Various international organizations have considered adopting standards for CSR, which already exist in various forms. The OECD's Guidelines for Multinational Corporations include standards for corporate behavior that amount to standards for CSR. As we saw in chapter 3, the Global Reporting Initiative is working hard to develop widely accepted universal systems for monitoring and reporting nonfinancial outcomes. And we have seen various sector-based efforts at developing guidelines for corporate behavior, for example, in forestry, garments and textiles, and mineral resource extraction.

In its initial review, the ISO's advisory group on social responsibility reported numerous definitions of social responsibility and corporate social responsibility, different forms of implementation, and varying levels of performance and compliance.[17] Even though the ISO's International Standard on social responsibility would be voluntary, it would, if adopted, likely force a high degree of convergence in international corporate social responsibility behavior across companies and countries. Critics of this approach will undoubtedly argue that standardization of efforts to improve social responsibility could lead to reductions in innovation by big companies and others. To this claim ISO would likely respond that its International Standards on environmental management (ISO 14000 series) have not had that effect.

## Box 4.3

### ISO's Push into Corporate Social Responsibility

At a meeting on June 24 and 25, 2004, in Stockholm, Sweden, ISO management agreed that ISO should develop an international standard for social responsibility. This decision followed from the ISO International Conference on Social Responsibility convened on June 21 and 22, 2004, by the Swedish Standards Institute. It was at this conference that 355 participants from 66 countries agreed to encourage ISO to proceed to develop an international standard on social responsibilty.

The conference reported broad agreement with the findings of an advisory group headed by a senior private-sector executive from Alcan of the United States. The advisory group was set up in early 2003 to begin deliberations, provide analysis, and map out the various worldwide social responsibility initiatives to determine whether there was a need for ISO involvement. Based on reported broad consensus at the conference, ISO management decided to proceed and created a dedicated working group to devise the social responsibility standard. This working group is to be jointly headed by the national standards institutes of Brazil and Sweden.

ISO reported that United Nations Secretary-General Mr. Kofi Annan welcomed this as "an initiative which dovetails well with the universal principles of the UN Global Compact on human rights, labour conditions, the environment and anticorruption." ISO expects to have the international standard completed by 2007. Although compliance is voluntary, ISO standards tend to become binding in business practice. ISO stated that "the work is intended to add value to, and not replace, existing intergovernmental agreements with relevance to social responsbility, such as the United Nations Universal Declaration of Human Rights, and those adopted by the International Labour Organization (ILO)."

SOURCES: ISO documentation and the online ISO Corporate Social Responsibility and Standards Forum.

Of course, numerous major global companies have gone ahead on their own, tailoring their approaches according to the advice of external and in-house CSR consultants. Royal Dutch Shell, for example, which was attacked in the late 1990s by a swarm of human rights groups for its ties to the dictatorship of General Sani Abacha in Nigeria, adopted a Statement of Business Principles that included consultation with NGOs.[18] Additionally, Shell spends some $80 million a year on social programs, hospitals, schools, and infrastructure in Nigeria. It regards this as filling a vacuum left by the national government. The trouble is that Shell is not the government; it lacks legitimacy. So its generosity is regularly under-appreciated. Recently Shell entered into a partnership with the United Nations Development Programme in Nigeria. Together they are helping to build and strengthen local government so that it has the capacity and resources to do what needs to be done and to ensure that the benefits of tax payments are felt locally.[19]

As CSR-type efforts by profit-seeking companies have expanded,[20] it is possible to identify some of the different types of "extracurricular" corporate activity that have arisen in the last decades and even in the last handful of years. This is illustrated in figure 4.1, which shows that contemporary MNCs in both developed- and developing-country contexts conduct numerous and varied activities beyond and linked to their core business activities. These activities, they contend to shareholders (and to respond to Friedman), are connected with the production of profits to varying degrees, either directly or indirectly, and in the short or long term. But sometimes, and increasingly, the connection can be quite tenuous and sometimes bewildering to a hard-nosed accountant. The connection of these activities and transactions to the business bottom line is also often viewed cynically by outside critics of MNCs. Examples of these activities include gifts to charity, financial support for a community event, protective workplace measures for employees, and publicity campaigns supporting social objectives. Some reasons a company might do any of these include, for example: to have a sense of benevolence; to improve brand and reputation; to ensure life-long recognition among a target group; to reduce country risk; or to satisfy staff.

In a developing-country context some of these actions would be more sustainable than others, some more poverty-reducing than others. In just about all cases the decisions made by company executives to approve these actions are based on judgment and experience rather than a provable financial model. This is one reason MNCs are these days placing renewed emphasis on general leadership and decision-making skills in managers. Inevitable questions from the MNCs which are devising appropriate or innovative CSR-type actions include: What are the benefits of involvement? What are the financial costs and the risks? Will involvement in one or more development projects detract from mainstream activities or core projects? Companies are increasingly perceiving these questions to be endogenous to their overall strategy rather than as exogenous considerations.

To illustrate the growing convergence of MNC interest in optimizing CSR activities, in September 2004 nine of the world's largest companies, including General Electric, IBM, and General Motors, together with the UK's not-for-profit consulting firm AccountAbility, joined together to identify the most effective and sustainable elements of corporate citizenship initiatives. The investigation is aimed especially at those elements of corporate social responsibility programs that add business value and, therefore, are sustainable and defensible in tough business cycles. Over the next three years the project will seek to:

a) Align corporate citizenship into the core business strategy by defining what activities are material to the company.
b) Respond to and learn from societal expectations in a manner that creates value for the business and stakeholders.
c) Align corporate citizenship values with operational excellence to ensure that ethics and the interests of good corporate governance are maintained.
d) Create opportunities for leadership that allow companies to influence the best practices of others.[21]

This sort of initiative by such large global corporations exemplifies MNCs' growing interest in using their CSR departments more efficiently, making the most of their CSR dollar, and ensuring that CSR has a sustainable impact. This is good news both for those who are generally disparaging of CSR as gimmicky and for those who want MNCs to do more. It shows that MNCs are alive to the possibilities, but also that they see the need for greater scientific review of different options to allow them to move forward with greater confidence.

One reason for the new business case for CSR is that companies and their financiers are increasingly seeing a link between intangible assets and shareholder value. It admittedly remains hard to value intangible assets, but it doesn't make the link with value any less real. The UK's *Financial Times* reported that a recent survey of European fund managers, investors, and financial analysts conducted by CSR consulting firms "suggested that most in the industry saw at least some link between intangible assets and shareholder value."[22] At the very least, the existence of some kind of link between what a corporation does indirectly (CSR-type activities) and its intangible value is no longer disputed. But modern financial models are not well equipped to determine the magnitude of its importance. Craig Mackenzie, the head of investor responsibility at Insight Investment, said that the link "is getting to the point where it has some credibility. It's absolutely clear that corporate earnings are affected by what you might call CSR (corporate social responsibility) performance in one way or another . . . (but) . . . it would be wrong to exaggerate how far we are along in understanding how CSR adds value." Mackenzie added that "you're now beginning to see the big sell-side analysts doing really serious broker research on these issues, which is a very strong sign of the seriousness with which it's taken."[23]

Milton Friedman and others, who believe that companies should be doing nothing but pursuing pure profit and following the law, struggle to see the business and economic justification for the many types of corporate activities that tend toward the left of figure 4.1. Thus, the argument is about what activities and factors are related to the production of pure profits. Proponents of the expanded, more responsible, more giving role of corporations are, therefore, trying to strengthen the business case for CSR, to make it more defensible, not least in order to give business managers a freer hand for some of the CSR initiatives that they would personally like to see their companies pursue. This is helpful because, the stronger the business case for CSR-type efforts, the easier it will be for individual managers to advocate their implementation. It is quite common for individual managers to have efficient and sustainable CSR initiatives in mind while lacking the ability to sell them internally due to the absence of a vigorous supporting business case.

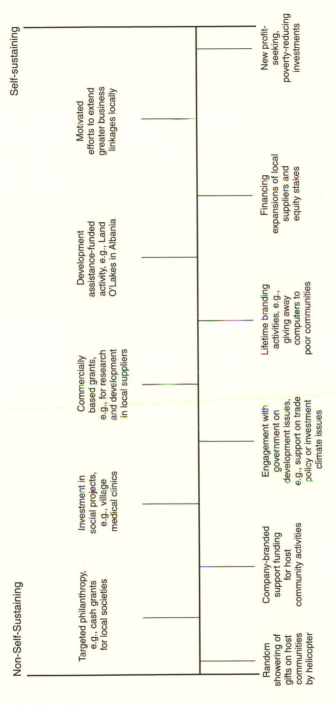

Non-Self-Sustaining

Self-sustaining

Targeted philanthropy, e.g., cash grants for local societies

Investment in social projects, e.g., village medical clinics

Commercially based grants, e.g., for research and development in local suppliers

Development assistance-funded activity, e.g., Land O'Lakes in Albania

Motivated efforts to extend greater business linkages locally

Random showering of gifts on host communities by helicopter

Company-branded support funding for host community activities

Engagement with government on development issues, e.g., support on trade policy or investment climate issues

Lifetime branding activities, e.g., giving away computers to poor communities

Financing expansions of local suppliers and equity stakes

New profit-seeking, poverty-reducing investments

Figure 4.1. Indirect, non-immediate, and non-mainstream activities by a developed country MNC operating in a developing country.

In what is a form of response to this conundrum, the Dutch government is undertaking research to establish a business case for CSR focused on all businesses, small and large. The anticipated set of voluntary principles would aim to:

(i) help entrepreneurs to develop their own ideas about
    corporate social responsibility and
(ii) provide an insight for social groups and government bodies
    as to what exactly may be expected from companies.[24]

National government regulations might be falling somewhat short of civil society calls for more corporate contributions to social objectives, but developed-country governments are invariably moving in that direction. Notably, aside from requiring adherence to the OECD guidelines on multinational corporations, the Dutch government's core business advice to its private sector is to be mindful of "people, planet, and profit."[25]

## The Disbelievers

There are many critics who are not wholly impressed by corporate social responsibility initiatives, either with the success of their implementation or the breadth of their acceptance by companies. In an Internet-based exchange called "Conversations with Disbelievers," a group of like-minded NGOs have attempted to assess systematically the corporate response to calls for more business activity on social issues. They have found that even though evidence for the business case for corporate responsibility is mounting, there is still much inertia on the part of companies. The disbelievers identified four principal reasons for this:

1. the evidential information on successful cases is deemed unreliable;
2. the evidence is irrelevant to key business objectives;
3. the sources of the evidence are not accepted as valid; and
4. the examples and arguments presented are incompatible with business decision-makers' extant attitudes.[26]

Interestingly, Conversations with Disbelievers found that there were three main reasons for corporate social programs:

1. pressure: a short-term need to respond to external pressures such as regulation or advocacy groups;
2. values: an expression of core values in the company; and
3. strategy: "corporate responsibility" supports or enhances a key long-term business strategy.[27]

In recent years there has been a shift toward the development of "partnerships" between big business and development institutions. This has come about for two main reasons:

(i) MNCs, although hearing the calls for greater involvement in development, recognize that they don't have the legitimacy to perform much of what is asked of them, and often they don't have the expertise.

(ii) International (governmental) development agencies realize they don't have the resources (their operating resources are, in fact, dwarfed by the private sector's) or a mechanism for making sustainable business-based improvements to people's lives.

Given these two reasons, we can begin to see the gap in the international development architecture to which we referred earlier. It involves the space that separates companies, development agencies, and nongovernmental organizations. To get a finer understanding of this disconnect, we will examine in the following chapter the range of governmental and intergovernmental agencies that are concerned both with MNCs and with poverty reduction.

## International Corporate Councils and Committees

Before moving on, however, we should quickly review some of the more important international business associations and forums that bring MNC managers together to discuss issues related to development: for example, the International Chamber of Commerce (ICC), the World Economic Forum, the Center for International Private Enterprise, and the World Business Council for Sustainable Development. These associations often share a variety of objectives ranging from advocacy on behalf of business to the promotion of good corporate behavior. But none harness MNC strengths for poverty reduction.

At their meetings they stress, for example, observing environmental standards, improving contract dispute mediation, reforming corporate governance, improving the mechanisms for business-government dialogue, and promoting the benefits that accrue from liberalized trade and investment and transfer of technology. This approach largely reflects the fact that during the 1980s and early 1990s the world's large companies were pressed by NGOs and their home and host governments to reduce their "footprint" and "do no harm." At the same time, MNCs everywhere were increasingly focusing on efficiency, applying new technologies, maximizing innovation, downsizing, and outsourcing. Thus, both companies and the relevant institutional infrastructure related to them were focused on fencing in effects and reducing impacts. In recent years, however, there has been a call, indeed a shout, for business to "do more," to expand its footprint, visibility, and impact with a strong emphasis on minimizing negative externalities and maximizing additional positive effects. This is illustrated in figure 6.2 in chapter 6.

## International Chamber of Commerce

The ICC is the world's leading association of international businesses. Founded in 1919 in Paris, the location of its current headquarters, it has established voluntary international standards for business sectors such as banking, trade, insurance, e-commerce, and shipping. It also houses the World Chambers Federation, the principal international association of chambers of commerce from around the world. It serves as an advocate for global business, is a strong believer in the benefits of globalization, provides arbitration services to resolve disputes, and holds regular conferences for its members.[28]

## World Economic Forum

The World Economic Forum began in 1970 in Davos, Switzerland, as a loose association of European businesspeople who met to discuss

pressing international issues of the day. It has grown over time in stat-
ure and its annual meetings now bring together an impressive array of
businesspeople, statesmen, and activists to discuss global business, social, and environmental matters. It maintains a broad interest in the
issue of globalization. Over time the World Economic Forum has
strengthened its convening power and now has an enviable record of
bringing together business and civil society in ways that reduce mutual
suspicion and strengthen their ability to work together. Its International Business Council considers various international business issues
and advises the World Economic Forum on possible solutions. The
Forum also maintains a Global Institute for Partnership and Governance that aims to broaden the applicability of the plethora of partner-
ship-type initiatives around the world. Apart from this and the IBC,
and its own influence over international corporate views, the World
Economic Forum has no concrete mechanism for harnessing the resources of MNCs for poverty reduction.

## World Business Council for Sustainable Development

Dating back to before the 1992 Rio Earth Summit, the World Business Council for Sustainable Development evolved into its current
form in 1995 following a merger between the original Business Council for Sustainable Development and the ICC-inspired World Industry
Council for the Environment. Although its origins are rooted in lessening the environmental impact of business, the WBCSD is now focused on the broader agenda of "sustainable development" and "sustainable livelihoods." With 170 major MNCs as members, together
with an extensive network of other interested companies and organizations, the WBCSD has come to play an important role in leading
thinking on the role of business in sustainable development. Based in
Geneva, it has produced a wealth of case studies and publications on
the business case for sustainable development. Nevertheless, even as it
provides useful networking opportunities and leadership on this issue,
it has devised no mechanism to facilitate MNCs' contributions to poverty reduction.

## Conclusion

This sketch of what business is doing to meet the challenges to its legitimacy and to more effectively serve societal goals shows unquestionable sensitivity to the problem. Yet it also reveals uncertainty, even anxiety, about what to do beyond attending meetings, making statements, signing protocols, and the like. Wise executives realize that their companies have the capacity and the power to make far greater contributions to global poverty reduction than they are now making. At the same time, they are mindful of their obligations to their shareholders, who are often largely retirees and pensioners. They don't like being portrayed as inherently bad, not when they are staffed by "people like you and me." MNC executives and staff largely see themselves as good and feel personal hurt at the attacks to which they are sometimes subjected. As Lord Browne said in his recent address to the Princeton Environmental Institute in defense of business:

> Business is not a passive force. Business is one of the most creative and progressive elements in society, providing the means and the choices which make human progress possible. That is true in terms of the environment and other social challenges. Business cannot take society's decisions, but we can provide the menu of choices. That's our distinctive role. And it is an honourable role. The caricature is that business is greedy, ruthless and unprincipled. Of course, you can find examples to prove that. Of course business makes mistakes. But business as a whole is an indispensable contributor to the continuing story of human progress. We invest to create new wealth. We take ideas and make them real. We take problems and work to find solutions. Those roles are unique to business. They are honourable activities and that's why I believe business at its best is an honourable and noble activity.[29]

MNCs need a way to reconcile these various forces and drivers and the threat posed to their legitimacy; they can do this by working to reduce global poverty, and measuring improvements, while at the same time meeting their obligations to show a profit.

The organizations described in this chapter make up that part of the international development architecture that business has created. In chapter 3 we described another part of that architecture: the NGOs. In the next chapter we shall review the remaining part, that which has been created by governments, and then go on to consider in some detail the nature of the problem of poverty and explore some options about how to deal with it more effectively.

# 5

# International Development Architecture

Numerous international governmental institutions address issues associated with globalization. They review, advocate, and analyze flows of foreign direct investment, portfolio investment, and debt capital as well as trade, the speculative exchange of foreign currencies, environmental, social, and cultural impact, and the transfer of technology. Some of these international institutions also seek to influence the role and behavior of multinational corporations, especially regarding corporate governance and environmental impact. In recent years most development organizations have given top priority to the reduction of global poverty. Despite all this, however, there is no single, universally accepted institution that has sought to harness the resources and capabilities of MNCs to reduce global poverty.

In this chapter we sketch the current structure of governmental agencies and organizations devoted to international development as related to MNCs. In so doing we shall reveal the gap that needs to be filled if progress is to be made toward meeting the widely endorsed Millennium Development Goals and reducing global poverty. (The MDGs are described in box 5.1.)

## Multilateral Governmental Agencies

International development agencies—owned, funded, and controlled by the governments of rich countries—are broadly concerned with development in general and poverty reduction in particular, but their connection to MNCs is weak and variable. These institutions, focused on reducing poverty and improving the capability of governments in developing countries to implement various development-related proj-

---

Box 5.1

**Millennium Development Goals**

In September 2000, world leaders gathered at the Millennium Summit at the United Nations General Assembly in New York. Following the meeting, the UN issued the "Millennium Declaration" with eight broad targets known as the Millennium Development Goals. These goals were adopted in order to place "development" at the heart of the world's political agenda. To monitor progress toward their fulfillment the UN initiated the Millennium Project, which examines implementation policy options, and the Millennium Campaign, which aims to build international political support for the MDGs.

The Millennium Development Goals:

1. To eradicate extreme poverty and hunger
2. To achieve universal primary education
3. To promote gender equality and empower women
4. To reduce child mortality
5. To improve maternal health
6. To combat HIV/AIDS, malaria, and other diseases
7. To ensure environmental sustainability
8. To develop a global partnership for development

---

ects, include the World Bank and its subsidiaries, the International Finance Corporation and Multilateral Investment Guarantee Agency, regional development banks such as the Asian Development Bank, the Organization for Economic Cooperation and Development, and various agencies of the United Nations family such as the International Labor Organization, United Nations Development Programme, United Nations Industrial Development Organization, United Nations Environment Programme, International Monetary Fund, and United Nations Conference on Trade and Development.

It is important to recognize that these organizations were established long before the rise to current prominence and strength of the modern

MNC. They were created during the final stages of World War II by those who were about to win, or well before in the case of the ILO. Their design was heavily influenced by the United States and the United Kingdom. Collectively, these organizations played an important role in sustaining the governments opposed to Soviet expansion during the Cold War. When that war ended in 1989/1991, these institutions sought a more varied set of goals bound up with the notion of development, but their structure and policies remained focused on working through recipient national governments. The disappointing results as far as poverty reduction is concerned are due partly to the fact that their client governments have often lacked either the desire or the ability to assist the poor who live within their borders.

Recently, these agencies, together with their NGO counterparts in civil society, have belatedly come to the realization that the power of MNCs can considerably augment their own disappointing efforts to reduce global poverty. Though NGOs and various development agencies have, over the last ten or so years, worked to develop more "partnerships" with business, they have failed to harness effectively the collective power of the MNCs.

Following are a few examples of initiatives and programs launched by international institutions to link with MNCs. The World Bank in the late 1990s started what it called the Business Partners for Development (BPD) program (see box 5.2). In 2002, the United Nations convened several international conferences, including the Financing for Development Conference held in Monterrey, Mexico, in 2002, at which the role of multinational corporations in promoting development was emphasized. In June 2004 in New York, the UN held its largest ever meeting with large and small companies that make up the membership of its Global Compact initiative. Both the UNDP and UNIDO have initiated ongoing business partnership programs that we shall discuss later. Suffice it to say here that although these various initiatives provide something of a touchstone for MNCs interested in development issues, they lack a sufficiently solid framework to facilitate greater interaction with international organizations and so cooperation on explicit poverty reduction issues remains limited.

The reason for the tenuous connections between MNCs and international development agencies is basically ideological in nature. Develop-

---

## Box 5.2

### Business Partners for Development

Business Partners for Development (BPD) was a time-bound, project-based initiative facilitated by the World Bank Group between 1998 and 2002 to help demonstrate the benefits that could flow from "tri-sector" partnerships between governments, business, and civil society. It focused on projects in just a few sectors and was mostly intended to produce a demonstration effect with a view to encouraging subsequent private replication by individual decision-makers. The four clusters of BPD activities were: Global Partnership for Youth Development; Global Road Safety Partnership; Natural Resources Cluster; and Water and Sanitation Cluster. It was one of the first real attempts to determine in a reasonably scientific way whether "partnerships" were as capable of delivering results as was being so widely suggested. The initiative mapped a range of partnership projects and was able to identify various common reasons for success and failure. Among other things, BPD found that partnerships are a good way of approaching erstwhile intractable problems and projects of high risk or complexity. BPD found that partnerships properly and voluntarily formed helped not only to spread risk, but also to share resources and skills. Importantly, successful partnerships often had a strong demonstration effect that could help to foster regular replication of successes.

SOURCE: The Knowledge Resources Group, Business Partners for Development, *Endearing Myths, Enduring Truths*, World Bank, 2002, and other seminars.

---

ment, however defined, is the province of government, so the traditional thinking goes. Business is and should be separate from government. Business is thus separate from development; it is devoted solely to increasing shareholder value. And in the eyes of many, with globalization this separation of roles has made business seemingly inimical to development. So any agency committed to development violates its imprimatur if it gets "too close" to business. The problem with this ideological formulation is that it defies reality and lessens the reduction of poverty.

Later we shall explore the meaning of the notion of development and poverty reduction in more detail, but, even using the term "poverty reduction" loosely to mean improved living standards, it is quite impossible to conceive of successful development without major business investment. Likewise, we know that in reality government and business are not separate. They are inevitably intertwined in countless ways for better or for worse; and therefore we know that in truth both are essential to development. We also know, however, that in many ways and in many places what passes for government is in no way an expression of what might be called the general will of the people. In many such cases NGOs present themselves as a form of pseudo-government. Thus, development is and must be the combined province of the confluence of government, NGOs, and corporations.

Let us now review some of the key elements of the international architecture as it relates to MNCs in an attempt to determine where there is traction on the issue of poverty reduction and where the gaps lie.

## The World Bank

The World Bank, also known as the International Bank for Reconstruction and Development (IBRD), is the world's central multilateral development agency. Its International Development Association deals with the poorest of its member countries. The World Bank lends and grants money to governments. It provides project loans, structural adjustment loans, technical assistance, policy advice, and knowledge services to poor and middle-income countries, all with the ultimate aim of reducing poverty.[1] It focuses on a wide range of sectors and activities, including, for example, social sector programs supporting health, education, youth, and gender; macroeconomic policy; public-sector reform; development of the private sector and anticorruption initiatives; civil society partnership; emergency management and disaster relief systems; environmental safeguards and programs; infrastructure improvements; and community development. The work of the other development banks—the Asian Development Bank, the African Development Bank, and the Inter-American Development Bank—follows similar approaches and agendas. The European Bank for Reconstruction and Development tends to focus more on private sector–related investments, having been set up in 1991 to bolster private markets in formerly communist-controlled European countries and former states of the collapsed Soviet Union.

The World Bank normally works with and through national governments or sometimes with subnational levels of government in developing countries. The Bank uses what it calls Poverty Reduction Strategy Papers to coordinate the programs, policies, and objectives of the client government, the Bank, and other donors and to link them to the goals of reducing poverty and improving living standards. These PRSPs are intended to help ensure that government policy-makers remember the poor. They are supposed to provide an umbrella framework for World Bank activity, including concessional financing, programs to increase domestic ownership of various development projects, and coordination of various donor and government programs. Preparation of PRSPs and related documents are, formally speaking, the responsibility of client governments. In practice, however, the World Bank and its sister agency, the IMF, provide considerable input and guidance during the preparation of PRSPs, depending on the capacity of the government and the strength of the working relationship between the Bank and the client.

The development of the private sector in all the World Bank's client countries is invariably a critical factor, if not *the* critical factor, in implementing a poverty-reduction strategy: the private sector after all is the key to the economic growth without which the poor will not improve their conditions and livelihoods. It is remarkable, therefore, that MNCs rarely, if ever, participate in the discussion, preparation, or drafting of these strategies. The World Bank's guidelines[2] on PRSPs do, however, make a reference to the need for consultation with local private-sector representatives through relevant chambers of commerce. But the world's largest corporations, the strongest engines of economic change and one of the key drivers of poverty reduction in developing countries, are largely left out of the process. So while the PRSP process is proving, since its inception in 1999, to be a useful framework for World Bank and IMF activity, the effective absence of MNCs from the process is puzzling and stands in stark relief to the involvement in the process of civil society NGOs.

One is forced to conclude that MNCs, despite their utility, are regarded as somehow illegitimate for the purposes at hand and are not to be trusted by governmental bodies focused on development. Their exclusion by development agencies reflects a broader problem of legitimacy that, as we shall see, has also affected UN relations with big companies. It seems a sad irony that the organizational entities most capable of reducing poverty in poor countries with a high degree of sustainability are excluded from efforts to do so.

Going beyond the PRSP mechanism, the World Bank as well as other international institutions also generally tend to ignore the specific role of MNCs in their broader development planning. Take as an example the Bank's World Development Report 2005. Adopting a well-chosen and important topic, the report focuses on the importance of investment climates in developing countries and how to improve them as a way of reducing poverty. The selection of this topic for the Bank's annual development report was a significant and welcome step to bring to the center of the development debate the role of investment and the factors that influence domestic private capital formation and flows and stocks of FDI. The report variously emphasizes improved policy-making and regulation as a way of assuring greater certainty for investors, foreign and domestic; better financial sector intermediation; better arbitration processes for business disputes; lower costs of doing business; and the lessening of corruption. It affirms that increasing investment is the best way to grow an economy and increase employment. In this context the report recalls that opinion surveys of poor people confirm that they view employment and the opportunity to generate income as the best way to begin to reduce their poverty.[3] The World Development Report 2005 also notes that foreign direct investment by MNCs can do much to improve a developing country's investment climate. Multinational corporations are, for example, often in the best position to make first-hand judgments about individual national investment climates, especially cross-country comparisons, and to provide sophisticated and informed analysis. Unfortunately, the report fails to take the logical next step. It fails, or is unable, to suggest a mechanism to provide a practical way for MNCs to contribute and play the constructive role of which they are capable.

One example of the World Bank's effort to work with the private sector to maximize poverty reduction is the so-called "Extractive Industry Review" (EIR). Launched in 2001 and completed two years later, the review, conducted by a select group of "eminent persons" from the developing world, made recommendations regarding the Group's involvement in the critical oil, gas, and mining sectors. The recommendations, which were generally endorsed by the World Bank's management in 2004, urged the Bank and the IFC to ensure that these industries, aside from limiting environmental damage and flooding the coffers of corrupt governments, do more to alleviate poverty.[4]

## The International Finance Corporation

The part of the World Bank that interacts most closely with MNCs is the International Finance Corporation. Established in 1956 to support private-sector objectives and referred to as the "private-sector arm" of the World Bank, the IFC has 176 member countries, the most recent entrant being East Timor (in 2004). Its main function is to invest in private, profit-making enterprises in developing countries using its own funds as well as syndicated loans. It does not initiate commercial projects but normally takes a minority equity or debt stake in them. The IFC responds to formal approaches from private companies, often large foreign investors wanting to do business in a developing country, and helps to finance these private business ventures, taking advantage of its convening power and honest-broker status. It also offers a range of technical advisory services to client governments.

The IFC and the World Bank's Foreign Investment Advisory Service (FIAS) offer advice to developing country governments on such topics as corporate social responsibility and investment climate improvements. The IFC also manages in developing countries worldwide a number of "project development facilities" which are designed to improve business development services and strengthen the investment climate, especially in support of domestic small and medium-sized enterprises.

In addition, the IFC recently established the Strengthening Grassroots Business Organizations Initiative (SGBI)[5] intended to target smaller, community-driven businesses. It rightly argues that such small businesses, especially in the least developed countries, are often the most effective way to meet the objectives of the local community. The IFC has correctly assessed that those countries with the greatest development challenges are where market failures are most pronounced, the need for intervention most defensible, and the positive impact of investment and business activity on poverty levels greatest. MNCs are unilaterally directing enormous volumes of FDI to, for example, China, India, the United Arab Emirates, and Mexico, but little or none to such countries as Haiti, Sudan, Yemen, Nepal, Guatemala, or Papua New Guinea. The IFC noted that the SGBI was initiated "to fill a gap in the product line of the World Bank Group" and to provide "economic opportunities for the poorest, in environments and segments where 'normal' private companies" are not investing.[6] (Box 5.3 contains an example of an SGBI project.)

The SGBI is a constructive acknowledgment of two things. First, the gap between the respective objectives of socially driven and profit-seeking businesses is reducing in size and, as we saw in chapter 3, is increasingly indistinguishable. Second, many poor economies still lack the large-scale employment opportunities brought about by FDI. This is because MNCs are often reluctant to invest in the poorest countries in which risks are high, obstacles numerous, and financial returns uncertain. We can see that a range of exogenous factors works against greater MNC investment in countries in which poverty is greatest. Lower investment levels by MNCs lead to fewer jobs, slower economic growth, and greater poverty.

Noting the costs to the poor countries of foregone investment, the IFC's SGBI wants to focus on providing technical skills and what it calls "patient" capital, which it describes as the critical but lacking ingredients. Patient capital, that is, capital with lower required rates of return and longer payback periods, is sorely needed to help drive sustainable poverty-reducing investment in the world's poorest places.

Although particularly useful, the fact that initiatives such as SGBI have arrived so late demonstrates the glaring absence of appropriate mechanisms within the international architecture to encourage private MNC investment in the world's poorest countries. The IFC, even as

Box 5.3

**Honey Care Africa and SGBI**

Honey Care Africa is one of the SGBI's pilot projects. The bee-keeping operation in Kenya is breaking new ground as a community-based, commercially oriented project. Established in 2000, Honey Care Africa manages community-kept bee hives and collects and sells honey. The project manages, on a cooperative basis, more than 17,000 hives and involves some 2,500 beekeepers. Because the project works at the grassroots level and has strong poverty-reducing characteristics but falls outside the scope of a normal commercial operation and thus has no ready access to regular sources of finance, it fell within the realm of the SGBI's mandate. SGBI intends to support Honey Care Africa through the direct infusion of "patient" capital, support for a more extensive marketing strategy, and technical support for its production facilities. SGBI also intends to assess the social and economic impact of the project across Kenya.

SOURCES: World Bank press release, Washington, D.C., June 25, 2004; and World Business Awards, Marrakech, June 8, 2004.

the World Bank's private-sector arm, does not lead in making private investments. It joins deals, helps with finance, works to spread risk, organizes insurance, and lessens the chance of expropriation of assets. But its mandate does not permit the IFC to go further in harnessing the strength of the world's largest companies to further drive global poverty reduction.

## The OECD

The Organization for Economic Cooperation and Development emerged in 1961 out of the former Organization for European Economic Cooperation, which was created after World War II to help administer the Marshall Plan. OECD programs cover a wide range of governance, macroeconomic, and industrial issues affecting its thirty rich country members and seventy poor country associated "nonmembers."[7] It conducts research and analysis and convenes meetings to encourage the adoption of accepted international standards and conventions. The OECD helps to shape the behavior of MNCs based in its member countries. It focuses on standards of corporate governance, rules of disclosure, anticorruption guidelines, and rules for insolvency.

In 1962 the OECD established the Business and Industry Advisory Committee. Although intended to facilitate private-sector contributions to OECD deliberations, in fact, member governments still tend to drive the BIAC agenda.

As we noted in chapter 3, in the late 1990s the OECD sought unsuccessfully to initiate a Multilateral Agreement on Investment, something akin to a worldwide generic set of rules for foreign investment. As noted earlier, it was shelved owing to uncertainty among OECD governments coupled with fierce opposition by a coalition of NGOs that saw the MAI as an assault on the environment, endangered species, and poor nations. The OECD nevertheless does have on its books the Declaration on International Investment and Guidelines for Multinational Enterprises, which seeks to enshrine minimum standards of investment and business behavior by MNCs based in OECD member countries. By requiring the same standards of behavior among all MNCs, the OECD has helped to level the playing field, lessen systemic corrupt payments, and minimize other damaging investment practices. The OECD Committee on International Investment and Multinational Enterprises can issue clarifications to the Declaration.

The OECD, perhaps ahead of other international institutions, is advocating an increased role for MNCs in development. Its 2002 report on maximizing the benefits of FDI in developing countries sets out some objectives and possibilities for ways to move ahead.[8] The report explicitly emphasized the broad and deep range of benefits FDI can bring to a poor country, at the same time recognizing that it has costs and might have negative side effects. The report noted that the positive spillovers of FDI "contribute to higher economic growth, which is the most potent tool for alleviating poverty in developing countries" and also lead to better domestic standards of corporate responsibility and environmental behavior.[9]

## The United Nations

The United Nations coordinates the activities of its various agencies and employs its strong convening capacity to pull together individuals and groups for discussion and agreement on policies and approaches. It is only in the most recent years that MNCs have been included in these discussions. As we noted earlier, it was not until 2002 that the UN convened the International Conference on Financing for Development in Monterrey, Mexico. This was the first major UN-led international summit meeting that squarely placed the issue of private financing at the center of the global development agenda.

The conference was called after economists noted the recent and abrupt changes in capital flows that started in the 1980s and have since continued. It had become readily apparent that flows of private capital, both portfolio and FDI, to developing countries had become larger than flows of debt capital or official development assistance. The meeting developed the "Monterrey Consensus," which set out a range of initiatives and objectives consistent with the achievement of poverty reduction and the other objectives of the UN's Millennium Development Goals. After affirming in Monterrey that inflows of foreign direct investment to developing countries, although not evenly spread, provided the bulk of external financing for the developing world, the conference encouraged MNCs to increase their investments in order to reduce global poverty. The implementation mechanisms required to accomplish this, however, were not established at Monterrey, nor have they been since, although the participants at the Monterrey conference did recognize the need for followup dialogue to monitor progress. In 2002, the UN also convened the World Summit for Sustainable Development in Johannesburg, South Africa, at which the role of multinational corporations in promoting development was emphasized. (See box 5.4 for a description of WSSD.)

Although the UN has not put in place mechanisms for developing significant ways and means to advance the Financing for Development

---

Box 5.4

**World Summit on Sustainable Development**

The World Summit on Sustainable Development (WSSD) was held in Johannesburg, South Africa, in August and September 2002. Following from the 1992 "Earth Summit" in Rio de Janeiro, Brazil, the WSSD brought together tens of thousands of participants from around the world, including representatives of governments, NGOs, development agencies, multinational corporations, and community groups. It focused world attention on development challenges and encouraged action to meet them. As part of WSSD, and together with the International Chamber of Commerce, the World Business Council for Sustainable Development used the occasion of WSSD to initiate "Business Action for Sustainable Development," a forum in which MNCs would meet to exchange ideas on global sustainable development issues. As it turned out, BASD was a one-time-only demonstration of commitment.

SOURCES: UN documentation on WSSD and comments from participants.

---

(FfD) agenda, the Monterrey Conference did put FDI and FfD "on the map" and has helped spawn a range of subsequent discussions and smaller conferences on the issue.[10]

The UN also runs the United Nations Research Institute for Social Development (UNRISD), which conducts research on contemporary issues affecting the development agenda, including a research project called "Business Responsibility for Sustainable Development." This project is producing a series of papers intended to encourage dialogue on the nexus between the corporate, social, and environmental responsibilities of MNCs and development. The research focuses on the following questions.

(i) Is the TNC (transnational corporation) discourse on "corporate responsibility" being applied in practice?
(ii) Where progress is apparent, what types of pressures, incentives, and institutional arrangements are promoting change?

(iii) Do voluntary initiatives and corporate self-regulation constitute effective alternatives to government and international
regulation?

(iv) What are the implications for development in poor countries
of efforts by TNCs and others to raise social and environmental standards?[11]

## The UN Global Compact

The UN's Global Compact has been extending its outreach to the
world's companies since its creation in 1999. Originally conceived by
the UN Secretary-General, Kofi Annan, the Global Compact was an
attempt to bring together the world's largest MNCs to encourage voluntary adoption of universal basic standards related to human rights,
the environment, and labor. The Global Compact is steered by five UN
agencies: the Office of the High Commissioner for Human Rights;
the UN Industrial Development Organization; the International Labor
Organization; the UN Development Programme; and the UN Environment Programme. As of mid-2004, more than 1,600 members had
joined, including several hundred major MNCs, medium-sized companies from the developed and developing worlds, and other groups such
as labor, human rights, and environmental NGOs.

The Global Compact is not a regulatory body. Rather, it has set up
a voluntary framework of principles to guide business action in developing countries. To avoid a free-rider problem, the Global Compact
encourages a system of reporting on member activities that adhere to
or advance the Global Compact's ten principles (see box 5.5).[12] NGOs
such as Amnesty International initially decried the initiative and then
proclaimed the need to place an independent observer within the
Global Compact office. An extension of Amnesty International's demand would logically seem to lead to a need to have observers in the
offices of Amnesty International.

It is worth noting that the establishment of the Global Compact
occurred soon after the unsuccessful attempt by the UNDP to establish the Global Sustainable Development Facility (see box 5.7) which
was designed to encourage UN collaboration with big business on
the broader development agenda. That effort was resisted by a number

## Box 5.5

### Global Compact Principles

*On Human Rights*

Principle 1  Businesses should support and respect the pro-
            tection of internationally proclaimed human
            rights.
Principle 2  Businesses should make sure that they are not
            complicit in human rights abuses.

*On Labor Standards*

Principle 3  Businesses should uphold the freedom of associ-
            ation and the effective recognition of the right
            to collective bargaining.
Principle 4  Businesses should uphold the elimination of all
            forms of forced and compulsory labor.
Principle 5  Businesses should uphold the effective abolition
            of child labor.
Principle 6  Businesses should uphold the elimination of
            discrimination in respect of employment and
            occupation.

*On Environment*

Principle 7  Businesses should support a precautionary
            approach to environmental challenges.
Principle 8  Businesses should undertake initiatives to
            promote greater environmental responsibility.
Principle 9  Businesses should encourage the development
            and diffusion of environmentally friendly
            technologies.

*On Anticorruption*

Principle 10  Businesses should work against all forms of
             corruption, including extortion and bribery.

SOURCE: UN Global Compact.

of major NGOs. They charged that the UNDP would be tainted by an association with MNCs. Eventually, the UNDP reversed itself and terminated the GSDF proposal. It was in this context that the Global Compact came into being, with a more modest agenda of voluntary compliance to agreed universal operating standards.

While the Global Compact's initial thrust was to minimize the negative impact of large corporations, it has now shifted to looking for ways in which corporations can make a greater positive contribution to development. This shift includes greater efforts to obtain the help of big business in meeting the Millennium Development Goals, the world's development experts having begun to realize that without a major effort by MNCs, the goals will not be reached.[13] This objective was implicit in the thrust of the UN Global Compact Leaders Summit held in New York on June 24, 2004.[14] As later reported in the *Washington International Business Report*, UN Secretary-General Kofi Annan spoke directly to the corporate CEOs participating in the Summit. "Perhaps no one has more at stake than the business community itself," he said.

> You have helped drive globalization. You have benefited greatly from it. Your vision, strategies, and organization embody it. And you have even more to hope for in the future. Yet our fragile global order stands in jeopardy today. Securing its future requires *your* resources and capacities, *your* advocacy, and *your* leadership. (The italics are Kofi Annan's.) It calls for the unique contributions that only private enterprise can make to the creation of public value, at home and abroad.[15]

Recognizing that business cannot be expected to provide all the solutions to the world's economic and social problems (as CEOs breathed a collective sigh of relief), the secretary-general insisted that business could make an essential contribution when governments provided the necessary structure and support.[16]

This change in thinking represents an important turning point at the UN and its development arm, the UNDP. They are beginning to realize that, putting ideology aside, MNCs are essential to development. Some of the outcomes of the June 2004 Global Compact meeting were extraordinary. For instance (in an echo of the IFC's Equator Principles), twenty major finance companies for the first time pledged to integrate social, environmental, and governance issues into their analysis of investment projects.[17]

Although business was being welcomed at the table, there was at the same time the sense that MNCs were the cause of much of the world's continued poverty. At the meeting, President Luis Inácio Lula da Silva of Brazil stated that business leaders must become "stronger advocates for the poor" and "lobby against agricultural subsidies."[18] This comment was reinforced by Kofi Annan, who added that "business must restrain itself from taking away, by its lobbying activities, what it offers through corporate responsibility and philanthropy." Of course, the UN Secretary-General was probably talking about just a handful of companies and, in fact, his comments on agricultural subsidies should be more squarely directed at the governments of the United States and the European Union. Indeed, it is worth recalling that at a 2004 conference in Marrakech a coalition of international business leaders strongly called for the resurrection of the Doha Development Agenda and an end to the U.S. and EU agricultural subsidies that adversely affect so many developing country agricultural sectors.[19] Business leaders, including global food companies such as Nestlé of Switzerland, looking at the general horizon of globalization, universally see intransigence on agriculture tariffs and subsidies by the European Union and the United States as one of the most important obstacles to be overcome.

## The United Nations Development Programme

The United Nations Development Programme, the development arm of the UN, focuses on crisis prevention and recovery, HIV/AIDS, poverty reduction, and democracy and governance. Its main asset is its worldwide network of country offices in more than one hundred member countries. Although it is not a funding organization like the World Bank or the other development banks, which means it is often unable to find the cash to run its programs and struggles to attain a reasonable level of effectiveness, the UNDP maintains the lead role in the UN's efforts to achieve the Millennium Development Goals.

Partnerships between the UNDP and leading MNCs to reduce poverty in developing countries is a particularly significant new development, suggesting a model for the future that we shall discuss in the final chapter of this book. A framework UNDP partnership, called Growing Sustainable Business for Poverty Reduction, sits alongside the UN Global Compact. The GSB initiative's purpose is to encourage and facilitate "greater private-sector contributions to poverty reduction and sustainable development through commercially viable activities." It seeks "increased investments and business activities in developing countries that link large companies to local small and medium enterprises, along with communities and other relevant partners."[20] As of April 2004, a small handful of projects were under way. In Ethiopia, Royal Dutch Shell with several local companies was establishing various solar-powered irrigation systems to benefit the country's rural economy. In Tanzania, ABB and Ericsson were exploring rural electrification and telecommunications projects, Kilombero Sugar and Tanga Cement were considering ventures that enabled farmers and small entrepreneurs to supply them with agricultural commodities and alternative fuels. EDF and Total were considering electrification projects in Madagascar and Unilever a project in Bangladesh.[21]

Under the GSB initiative, these global giants have agreed to explore and pursue commercially viable projects that have maximum impact on poverty reduction in the world's poorest countries. Such projects will undoubtedly require public-sector financing in their early stages as well as the cooperation and participation of local government and business. Although this initiative is entirely sensible, and in fact is the only conceivable way in which poverty in the least developed countries can be reduced, it is fraught with legitimacy problems requiring the most careful attention to governance. Thus, the role of the UNDP as guide and facilitator is essential, as are the participation and endorsement of an array of NGOs and international observers: CARE, Oxfam, and the International Confederation of Free Trade Unions (ICFTU).

It is noteworthy that no U.S. company is yet involved in the GSB initiative and U.S. participation in the Global Compact is highly limited. Some argue that this is a result of the emphasis U.S. companies, as opposed to their counterparts elsewhere, place on short-run returns to shareholders, while others attribute it to a view among American managers that "development" is the business of government.

Apart from GSB, an increasing number of MNCs are seeing great value in entering into partnership projects with UNDP and development agencies in a developing country. U.S. software giant Cisco, for example, has for some years made good use of UNDP's field offices to establish in some eighty countries "Networking Academies" to train local people in installing, operating, and maintaining routers and servers. These products, manufactured by Cisco, are essential to operating computer networks. (Box 5.6 includes other examples of global businesses that have partnered with UNDP.)

UNDP officials privately (when certain NGOs are not listening) attach great value to these partnership projects because they recognize that MNCs bring a high level of commitment and competency, technical skills, and resources that help the UNDP achieve its own varied development objectives. The UNDP supplies its own skills in project design, its main contribution perhaps being the legitimacy it provides and its ability to function as an "honest broker" between the government, community groups, local business, and the MNCs.

The UNDP, as it increasingly recognizes the potential potency of partnering with major multinational corporations, has begun to delineate common roles MNCs can play when partnering in development projects. These include providing financial support, project design services, and monitoring and evaluation; facilitating access to commercial credit; integrating with supply chains; supporting development of new local business models; and transferring skills and expertise to local clients.[22]

### The 1998 Fiasco and the Corporate Taint

The wonder is that it has taken the UNDP and MNCs so long to begin to get together and that the connection is so slight. To understand the timidity of the UNDP, it is helpful to look at the last time it tried to establish a private-sector affiliation in 1998. As we noted earlier, the UNDP had to abort an effort to establish a so-called "Global Sustainable Development Facility" designed to encourage MNCs to support some of UNDP's development objectives. This effort was howled down by a gaggle of NGOs arguing that MNCs did not have the "right" (read legitimacy) or mandate to undertake such initiatives with the UNDP. In the

## Box 5.6

### Examples of Private Partners in UNDP Development Projects

- Chevron-Texaco, Citibank, and UNDP have started the Atyrau Business Advisory Center in Kazakhstan, which provides training and access to credit. The center has helped local SMEs produce 280 business plans and access more than $2 million in loans and has more than 1,000 ongoing clients.
- Firestone, 3M, several large Mexican companies, and UNDP have initiated a supply-chain project to provide technical assistance to local SME suppliers in Mexico. The project aims to build the capacity of smaller local suppliers to better enable them to successfully provide supplies on an ongoing basis to larger corporations.
- Chevron-Texaco and UNDP launched the Angola Enterprise Fund in 2002, which is intended to provide training and incubation support to small businesses in Angola as well as various vocational training courses. Part of Chevron-Texaco's overall corporate effort in Angola, the intention is to invest a total of $10 million, with cofinancing from UNDP and other private businesses.

In all cases assessments of the partnerships showed that the participating MNCs were likely to accrue substantial political and brand benefits, the host governments to benefit via the social dividends obtained by their citizens, and the UNDP to find the activity in accordance with its "mandate to help countries promote sustainable human development" and with Millennium Development Goal No. 1 concerning the eradication of extreme poverty.

SOURCE: UNDP Working Document, "Supporting SME Entrepreneurship for Sustainable Development," February 2004.

words of one observer whom we interviewed: "NGOs feared that MNCs would infect the development work of the more respectable and benevolent UNDP." (Box 5.7 details the fate of the GSDF proposal.)

As we mentioned earlier, another relevant UNDP initiative was the recent formation of the Commission on the Private Sector and Development.[23] The Commission, convened during 2003, produced a report in early 2004 that emphasized the importance of attracting foreign investment to poor countries and making the distribution of the benefits of FDI more equitable within the country. Although its overall focus was on the domestic, often informal, elements of developing countries' private sectors, the report spoke of the need to "unleash" the potential of local micro-entrepreneurs and small and medium-sized enterprises and to reduce their costs of doing business and the barriers to entry they face. It also hinted at the imperative to develop mechanisms to capture the resources and willingness of MNCs to contribute more effectively to global poverty reduction. It went on to discuss the role of MNCs in helping small domestic businesses grow and prosper and sell their goods and services to the poor, referring to C. K. Prahalad's suggestion[24] to global companies to market more effectively to the world's poor. As an example of how far the debate on the role of big companies in the developing world has shifted—from impact minimization to outcome maximization (see figure 6.2 in the next chapter)—the UNDP report suggested "creating a scorecard to measure the success of multinationals and other large firms in creating profitable markets from poor consumers."[25]

Unfortunately, the Commission's report completely failed to spell out how its recommendations were going to be implemented. There were no suggestions whatsoever regarding ways in which the resources and capabilities of MNCs could be brought to bear more effectively on poverty reduction. There was not even an endorsement of the UNDP's own GSB program, referred to above, nor recommendations for its advancement. Nevertheless and importantly, the leaders of the Group of Eight[26] at their meeting at Sea Island, Georgia, in the United States in June 2004 subsequently endorsed the recommendations in the report and committed their governments, through "a dedicated Action Plan," to support a range of initiatives focused on the private sector.[27]

Box 5.7

## UNDP's 1998 Proposal for a
## "Global Sustainable Development Facility"

The proposal was initiated internally by the UNDP early in 1998. A UNDP project manager was appointed and interest was solicited from a range of major global corporations. By July 1998, eleven corporations had agreed to participate in the feasibility phase of the Global Sustainable Development Facility (GSDF). These included Ikea and Ericsson of Sweden, Rio Tinto of the United Kingdom and Australia, Citibank of the United States, and Statoil of Norway. UNDP proceeded to design potential projects and appoint advisers to the project Steering Committee. Planning commenced for a project launch in mid-1999 following completion of the feasibility phase.

During the feasibility phase the GSDF initiative was described by UNDP as follows: "The Global Sustainable Development Facility project is an initiative that brings together leading global corporations and the UNDP to jointly define and implement a new facility to eradicate poverty, create sustainable economic growth, and allow the private sector to prosper through the inclusion of two billion new people in the global market economy. The first of its kind, this new initiative will bring UNDP's universality, forty years of development experience, and a network of offices in developing countries together with the knowledge and resources of the private sector."

Ultimately, the launch was aborted. The GSDF had intended to involve corporations fully and formally in major development initiatives. The GSDF had been proposed as an independent legal entity, governed and capitalized by corporate partners, operating within agreed UN development parameters. UNDP senior officials, in the face of fierce criticism from NGO partners, shelved the GSDF proposal.

SOURCES: Interviews with various UNDP staff; a UNDP GSDF launch preparation document; and reports from CorpWatch.org.

## The United Nations Conference on Trade and Development

The UN Conference on Trade and Development was established in 1964. As its name suggests, its core task is to improve the results that flow from trade. But UNCTAD also works on the interrelated issues of investment, technology, finance, and sustainable development. It seeks to promote trade and help bring the benefits of globalization to developing countries. UNCTAD closely follows the behavior and impact of MNCs, having in 1993 subsumed the role and functions of the former United Nations Center on Transnational Corporations (UNCTC).

In a recent report, UNCTAD[28] underscored the benefits that can flow to developing countries from liberalized trade. UNCTAD also produces the annual World Investment Report, which highlights links between FDI and development. UNCTAD has a strong analytical focus and produces some particularly useful research and data on issues related to globalization and international trade and investment. It also provides technical assistance to developing countries on issues such as bilateral investment treaties and technical trade matters. But UNCTAD has no effective mechanism to help MNCs become more directly involved in poverty reduction.

## The United Nations Industrial Development Organization

The UN Industrial Development Organization[29] was established in 1966 and became a specialized UN agency in 1985. UNIDO's main function, as set out in its strategy for 2004–7, "rests on the premise . . . that productivity enhancement plays a crucial role in promoting faster growth."[30] UNIDO therefore works to reinforce the benefits that come from the "multiple links between entrepreneurship, technology, productivity enhancement and growth."[31] To achieve this, UNIDO divides its work in a unique fashion into three distinct parts, which it calls "competitive economy, sound environment and productive employment." Accordingly, it has responsibility for a specific piece of the "development pie." To help it go about its work, UNIDO also has its own business partnership program, formed in 2000 after the creation of the

Global Compact. UNIDO seeks out productivity-improving partner-ship projects, such as, for example, a partnership project in Morocco with UNEP and BASF AG of Germany aimed at improving the eco-efficiency of a textile dye factory.

## National Government Organizations

The efforts of developed-country governments to enlist their corporate sectors in the cause of development are surprisingly limited. They all operate their own bilateral development agencies, for example, the Japan International Cooperation Agency (JICA), the Australian aid agency, AusAID, and the Swedish international aid agency, Sida. National governments also channel considerable development resources through the various international development organizations.

In chapter 3 we mentioned the Center for Global Development's CDI Index. The country that performed best in that index's investment category was The Netherlands. This was due at least in part to the Dutch government attaching CSR requirements to its outward investment promotion and export credit programs. This meant that a Dutch company applying for those government-provided services would need to include in its application details on, for example, policies to fight corruption, impact on the labor market, impact on the foreign economy, and the company's effects on the environment. The Dutch government was the only one found to have made explicit reference to the connection between FDI sourced from Dutch companies and poverty reduction in developing countries. But the details and mechanism used to achieve this are unclear. The Dutch government did note the following in its submission to the 2003 European Conference on Corporate Social Responsibility:

> Besides the benefit that FDI can bring to developing countries (the Government) also look(s) for companies to develop partnerships against poverty. This means partnerships with local communities, institutions and NGOs. Companies need to be aware of the impact of their activities on the local community. They can contribute to a better enabling environment for local business and contribute to the awareness of CSR issues.[32]

Many of the rich country governments have, over the last decade or so, sought to have a hand in regularizing CSR practices in some form. For example, in 2003 the European Union held its third "European Conference on Corporate Social Responsibility: The Role of Public Policies in Promoting CSR."[33] The conference considered experiences with CSR among member states with a view to creating a more "efficient social protection system" as a tool for enhanced competition and to strengthen the protection of the environment and human rights. The conferences are decidedly focused inward on matters that affect the EU, especially related to EU labor issues, rather than focused on poverty reduction in the world's developing countries.

A number of rich country governments, of course, have extensive foreign aid programs, some of which involve MNCs. For example, USAID has contracted the dairy cooperative, Land O'Lakes, to establish dairy industries in twenty-four developing countries. In Albania some eight thousand dairy farmers have been organized, trained, and assisted to start many small cooperatives and milk distribution facilities. USAID also has a Global Development Alliance (GDA) program under which it joins with some thirty MNCs, most of them based in the United States, to assist developing countries to stimulate local business development, improve health and education, protect the environment, and more. Home Depot, the U.S. hardware store chain, for example, is helping to encourage sustainable forestry practices. The U.S. company Chevron Texaco is helping in Angola with a series of projects designed to strengthen small and medium-sized businesses ($10 million per project over five years). Fludor and USAID are helping with sunflower oil processing in Benin (providing $838,000 and $320,000, respectively). And Coca-Cola and Motorola have teamed up to improve access to education for Moroccan girls. In 2003 the GDA was involved in more than two thousand alliance projects which, with leveraged private contributions, valued the portfolio of activities in excess of $2 billion.[34] Apart from USAID's GDA and Germany's Public-Private Partnership Programme, the United Kingdom has an initiative called the Business Linkages Challenge Fund, which also aims to make partnership arrangements with big business. This fund requires that projects be commercially viable, contribute broader development dividends, and have a positive impact on the poor.[35]

Various developed-country national governments now require their companies to augment their financial statements with sustainability reports. France introduced a law in 2001 that requires French companies to report annually on the social, economic, and environmental consequences of their activities. The French government, recognizing the radical nature of its requirement, provides companies with a suggested format and coverage and is currently assessing the workability and utility of the law. Initial assessment suggests that the requirement has had a strong effect on company reporting and has also influenced investors' and credit rating agencies' perceptions of companies.[36]

## Conclusion

Against the backdrop of this international architecture, corporate managers are being prodded by NGOs, development professionals, the media, their own staff, and even idealistic shareholders to play a greater role in reducing global poverty. At the same time, MNCs firmly believe they are already doing a lot in the regular course of their business activity.[37] As noted earlier, the Monterrey Conference in March 2002 confirmed that the value of FDI channeled into developing countries by MNCs greatly exceeds the flow of, and creates more jobs than, official development assistance (which is often unsustainable), or the flow of debt capital (which again is often unsustainable, especially for funded projects not directly linked to generated revenues to repay the loans). The problem is that FDI inflows to developing countries and the benefits that flow from them are not evenly spread among or within developing countries. Many of the poorer developing countries are missing out. The poorest are remaining poor. This is a clear form of market failure. One of our purposes in writing this book is to show how this unevenness can be redressed.

Earlier in this chapter we mentioned a gap in the structure of international agencies vis-à-vis multinational corporations and programs aimed at poverty reduction. We have found that the various international development agencies do, in varying ways, consider the implications of globalization. And, as we shall see in the next chapter, they have collectively adopted the overarching goal of global poverty reduction. But they have not, for the different reasons we have discussed, latched their efforts and objectives on to the immense resources, capabilities, and goodwill of the world's global corporations. This is despite growing recognition among development practitioners that the capabilities of the world's MNCs are indispensable to poverty reduction. There exist no mechanisms through which those capabilities can be fully brought to bear in the world's poorest countries. MNCs need practical means through which they can more effectively reduce global poverty and revive their eroding legitimacy while maintaining earnings and an acceptable return on their investments.

Before discussing what those means are, in chapter 6 we shall analyze the nature of poverty itself and offer some thoughts about its alleviation. Then, in chapter 7, we shall explore the desires of the world's biggest and best businesses to contribute to poverty reduction, provide examples of their success, and suggest that effectiveness against this objective requires consistency with the firms' own long-term commercial interests.

# 6

# The Emerging International Consensus

World leaders like Kofi Annan and George W. Bush are undoubtedly sincere when they repeatedly say that reducing world poverty is of utmost importance. The problem is it won't be achieved under the current approach, and, since poverty is the seedbed from which political instability and terrorism grow, both can be expected to worsen unless something new is tried and succeeds. To quote Annan, "Poor nations left to collapse into conflict and anarchy are likely to become a menace to their neighbors and potentially—as the events of September 11 so brutally remind us—a threat to global security."[1] Terrorism flourishes among those who think they have nothing to lose and much to gain from reallocating power in the world.

Global demographics trends are not encouraging, as two scholars with the Brookings Institution have shown. "In the next fifty years," they write, "the world's population will increase by 50 percent from six billion to nine billion." The number of people living in the advanced industrial countries will remain about the same at roughly one billion— the increase will come entirely in developing countries. By 2050, people in developing countries will total about 90 percent of humanity.[2]

Much is at stake for global corporations in this context because, fairly or not, they receive a good portion of the blame for world poverty. They are after all the engines of globalization, and globalization has not only failed to reduce poverty, it has also increased the gap between the world's richest and poorest people. In the words of John Browne, chief executive of BP, one of the world's largest companies operating in some one hundred countries, there is a "climate of mistrust surrounding big business." Several years ago at the Harvard Business School he spoke of the fear that "such concentrated power is unconstrained," adding that, if business is to be trusted, "companies have to demonstrate that our presence, particularly in the poorer countries . . . is a source of human progress."

World concern about poverty is increasing not because of a sudden upsurge in morality but because the trend toward increasing globalization has revealed beyond a shadow of a doubt that the poor are a menace to the prosperous.

The vast majority of international financial institutions as well as other international organizations now refer to the reduction of global poverty as either their central objective or, at the very least, one of their key areas of concern and activity. Among all development agencies and international financial institutions, the World Bank has placed itself at the center of the international charge against global poverty, adopting as its mission statement, "Our dream is a world free of poverty." But the World Bank is not alone in this view. Virtually every international development organization is adopting this objective, in whole or in part, at least ostensibly.

This overwhelming breadth of international consensus across countries and institutions on the need to reduce global poverty is extraordinary, if only because this consensus has been reached only in the last twenty or so years. Recognizing the myriad moral, social, political, and economic imperatives driving the adoption of this agenda is not difficult. One key problem, however, is the simple fact that the characteristics and manifestations of poverty are intractable, complex, and varied.

In seeking to define the problem, most definitions of poverty tend to center around access to income, services, social safety nets, land, household security, and opportunity. A poverty level, in fact, a poverty threshold is, in turn, normally based on minimum levels of income or consumption represented in monetary terms. Poverty levels are set in various country contexts using different "baskets" of goods and services, taking into account changes over time and varying cultural and societal norms. The content and prices of these baskets, and the income levels of the population, are recorded and calculated using a laborious system of surveys, interviews, statistics, and various subjective assessments.

The affordability of these prescribed baskets helps to determine where the poverty line for a given country should be set. For example, the poverty line in East Timor was set in 2002 at just US$0.55 per day,[3] whereas in richer developing countries it is set at much higher rates. To obtain a picture of overall global poverty levels, the various national poverty statistics are collated and compared using prices at a base year to convert local currencies into one currency, the U.S. dollar. This process has allowed good measurement and comparisons of trends over time, with US$1 and US$2 a day now the most commonly used thresholds.[4] Excluding the people of rich countries, the essential state of global poverty among the world's six billion people, based on the figures[5] of 2001, which compare against the figures of 1981, is as follows:

- One-sixth of the world's population lives on less than US$1 a day, the total number of people living on less than US$1 a day having fallen from 1.5 billion in 1981 to 1.1 billion in 2001.
- More disturbingly, almost half of the world's population lives on less than US$2 a day, the total number of people living on less than US$2 a day having risen since 1981 from 2.4 billion to 2.7 billion.
- The percentage of the world's population living on less than US$1 a day has almost halved from 39.5 percent to 21.3 percent.
- The percentage of the world's population living on less than US$2 a day has fallen from 65.9 percent to 52.8 percent.
- If the incredible improvements in living standards in China were excluded from this worldwide data, the picture of global poverty would look very much worse. Figure 6.1 makes clear the effect improvements in living standards in the East Asia region have had on global poverty.

The factors that have driven the overall improvements in global poverty over the last twenty years are too extensive for singular treatment here. It is clear, however, that much of the improvement is linked to improved economic governance and liberalized approaches to trade and investment. But it is also clear that these improvements have not been great enough. As the World Development Indicators 2004 stated, "To achieve and sustain the levels of economic growth needed to reduce poverty, developing countries need greater access to foreign markets."[6]

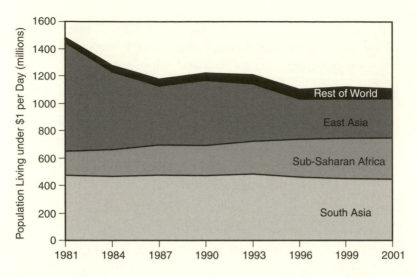

Figure 6.1. Numbers of poor by region ($1 per day). Source: World Bank, *World Development Indicators* 2004.

Table 6.1 shows the latest overall global poverty statistics, incorporating comparisons from 1981.

Unfortunately, current approaches to defeating poverty and all its elements are not succeeding. The international development community, which has adopted the reduction of developing country poverty as its overriding goal, has enshrined this in acceptance of the first Millennium Development Goal (see box 5.1) as its collective benchmark. Target 1, contained within the first MDG, is to "halve, between 1990 and 2015, the proportion of people whose income is less than one dollar a day." In a recent report updating the international development community's efforts against the various MDGs, the overall outlook was reported to be bleak.[7] The report stated that it was possible that the goal of halving the number of people living below the $1 a day level could conceivably be met by 2015, but noted that this is because of considerable economic success in China and India, the world's two most populous countries,[8] where, as Michael Klein, chief economist at the IFC, has pointed out, the poverty decline is due to the vigor of the private sector.[9] Elsewhere the problem of absolute poverty remains or has worsened and the worldwide problem of those living on less than $2 a day also persists.

TABLE 6.1
**New Poverty Estimates Trace the Decline of
Global Poverty since 1981**

| *People living on less than $1 a day (millions)* | | | | | | | |
| Region | 1981 | 1984 | 1987 | 1990 | 1993 | 1996 | 1999 | 2001 |
|---|---|---|---|---|---|---|---|---|
| East Asia & Pacific | 767 | 558 | 424 | 472 | 416 | 287 | 282 | 284 |
| China | 606 | 421 | 308 | 377 | 336 | 212 | 224 | 212 |
| Europe & Central Asia | 1 | 1 | 2 | 2 | 17 | 20 | 30 | 18 |
| Latin America & Caribbean | 36 | 46 | 45 | 49 | 52 | 52 | 54 | 50 |
| Middle East & North Africa | 9 | 8 | 7 | 6 | 4 | 5 | 8 | 7 |
| South Asia | 475 | 460 | 473 | 462 | 476 | 441 | 453 | 428 |
| ++Sub-Saharan Africa | 164 | 198 | 219 | 227 | 241 | 269 | 292 | 314 |
| Total | 1,451 | 1,272 | 1,169 | 1,219 | 1,206 | 1,075 | 1,117 | 1,101 |

| *Share of people living on less than $1 a day (%)* | | | | | | | |
| Region | 1981 | 1984 | 1987 | 1990 | 1993 | 1996 | 1999 | 2001 |
|---|---|---|---|---|---|---|---|---|
| East Asia & Pacific | 55.6 | 38.6 | 27.9 | 29.6 | 25.0 | 16.6 | 15.7 | 15.6 |
| China | 61.0 | 40.6 | 28.3 | 33.0 | 28.4 | 17.4 | 17.8 | 16.6 |
| Europe & Central Asia | 0.3 | 0.3 | 0.4 | 0.5 | 3.7 | 4.2 | 6.2 | 3.7 |
| Latin America & Caribbean | 9.7 | 11.8 | 10.9 | 11.3 | 11.3 | 10.7 | 10.5 | 9.5 |
| Middle East & North Africa | 5.1 | 3.8 | 3.2 | 2.3 | 1.6 | 2.0 | 2.6 | 2.4 |
| South Asia | 51.5 | 46.8 | 45.0 | 41.3 | 40.1 | 35.1 | 34.0 | 31.1 |
| ++Sub-Saharan Africa | 41.6 | 46.3 | 46.8 | 44.6 | 43.7 | 45.3 | 45.4 | 46.5 |
| Total | 39.5 | 32.7 | 28.4 | 27.9 | 26.2 | 22.3 | 22.2 | 21.3 |

| *People living on less than $2 a day (millions)* | | | | | | | |
| Region | 1981 | 1984 | 1987 | 1990 | 1993 | 1996 | 1999 | 2001 |
|---|---|---|---|---|---|---|---|---|
| East Asia & Pacific | 1,151 | 1,104 | 1,024 | 1,117 | 1,080 | 922 | 900 | 868 |
| China | 858 | 809 | 732 | 830 | 807 | 650 | 630 | 596 |
| Europe & Central Asia | 8 | 9 | 8 | 58 | 78 | 97 | 111 | 93 |
| Latin America & Caribbean | 99 | 119 | 115 | 125 | 136 | 117 | 127 | 128 |
| Middle East & North Africa | 52 | 50 | 53 | 51 | 52 | 61 | 70 | 70 |
| South Asia | 821 | 859 | 911 | 958 | 1,005 | 1,022 | 1,034 | 1,059 |
| ++Sub-Saharan Africa | 288 | 326 | 355 | 382 | 409 | 445 | 487 | 514 |
| Total | 2,419 | 2,466 | 2,466 | 2,689 | 2,759 | 2,655 | 2,730 | 2,733 |

SOURCE: World Bank, *World Development Indicators* 2004.

TABLE 6.1 (cont'd)

| Share of people living on less than $2 a day (%) | | | | | | | |
| Region | 1981 | 1984 | 1987 | 1990 | 1993 | 1996 | 1999 | 2001 |
| --- | --- | --- | --- | --- | --- | --- | --- | --- |
| East Asia & Pacific | 83.4 | 76.3 | 67.4 | 69.9 | 64.8 | 53.3 | 50.3 | 47.6 |
| China | 86.3 | 78.0 | 67.0 | 72.6 | 68.1 | 53.4 | 50.1 | 46.7 |
| Europe & Central Asia | 1.9 | 2.0 | 1.7 | 12.3 | 16.6 | 20.6 | 23.5 | 19.7 |
| Latin America & Caribbean | 26.9 | 30.4 | 27.8 | 28.4 | 29.5 | 24.1 | 25.1 | 24.5 |
| Middle East & North Africa | 28.9 | 25.2 | 24.2 | 21.4 | 20.2 | 22.3 | 24.3 | 23.2 |
| South Asia | 89.1 | 87.2 | 86.7 | 85.5 | 84.5 | 81.2 | 77.7 | 76.9 |
| ++Sub-Saharan Africa | 73.3 | 76.1 | 76.1 | 75.0 | 74.3 | 74.8 | 75.7 | 76.3 |
| Total | 65.9 | 63.4 | 59.8 | 61.6 | 60.1 | 55.3 | 54.2 | 52.8 |

SOURCE: World Bank, *World Development Indicators* 2004.

## Poverty and the Meaning of "Development"

The need for more effective corporate involvement in the fight against poverty stems from two factors: the inadequacy of government, and the nature of the system in which the poor are enmeshed.

### *The Government Problem*

One might wonder, despite the more than $1 trillion that has been spent on foreign aid since the end of World War II, why so little progress has been made. The reason is faulty assumptions by those in charge of "development" in the United States and other rich countries. Postwar financial assistance to countries devastated by conflict—Europe, Japan, South Korea, and Taiwan, for example—was effective because there were political and social institutions and governmental infrastructure in those countries ready and able to use that assistance to build a successful and competitive economy that dramatically reduced poverty. And, as in China, Singapore, and other Asian countries, a small amount of development assistance acted to prime the pump of domestic savings and investment and to attract additional foreign investment. Furthermore, the governments of these countries designed effective strategies for competing in the world. These strategies frequently violated the current dogmas of mainstream Western economists, calling for governmental subsidies, trade protection of key industries, and credit allocation so that the industries that flourished were those that could sustain a high living standard. It is ironic today to look back at the advice the U.S. economists gave postwar Japan: concentrate on small, labor-intensive businesses to absorb the unemployed, lower your trade barriers, and make use of your comparative advantage, which was cheap labor. Japan's heretical reply was: We intend to *create* our comparative advantage so that our people have high incomes by saving and investing in targeted industries with government and business working together.

Having observed the success in those countries that had been devastated by World War II, the development experts focused their attention on the rest of the world, supposing that grants and loans to governments would result in something called development, including poverty reduction. The problem was that many of those governments lacked either the desire or the capability to reduce poverty. Aid to many such governments actually worsened the plight of the poor by sustaining the political and social systems that caused their misery in the first place. This error has been repeated many times over in the postwar era, Latin America and Africa having suffered the most. During the Cold War, however, this discrepancy did not matter to the Washington planners; the United States and its allies were concerned with sustaining anti-Soviet regimes, not raising living standards.

With the end of the Cold War, at the World Bank and elsewhere, poverty reduction became goal number 1. But the notion of how to deal with it remained much the same as before, cemented in huge bureaucracies that preached a laissez-faire ideology called "the Washington consensus" and channeled money into governments, however mismanaged they might be. With the money came advice, conditions really, requiring commitment to the virtues of free trade, free markets, private enterprise, and the limited state. The result was that by 2004 in many countries, perhaps seventy or more, foreign aid had nourished the status quo but done little to reduce poverty.[10]

Several years ago the World Bank sent one of the authors to Kazakhstan to assist the Minister of Planning with the drafting of an economic strategy for the country. Kazakhstan is huge, five times the size of France, with a dwindling population of some 18 million. In Soviet days it was relatively prosperous, sustained by a network of weapons factories and space exploration installations. It is rich in mineral resources, including oil and many precious metals that foreign companies were quick to exploit following independence in 1991. Although the country's ruling circles have prospered, 80 percent of the population living in the countryside slipped into poverty. The country's wealth had not reached them.

In the Soviet days the rural people worked huge collective farms, producing wheat and other grains. Sustained by $10 billion per year in subsidies from the old USSR, these collectives also provided schools, health facilities, and other social services. When the subsidies stopped, the collectives collapsed. U.S. aid and World Bank loans were accompanied by advice that the planning minister felt constrained to take: break up the collectives, introduce property rights, provide farmers with their own farms, and let them sell in the open market and competition among them will ensure the best results. The only problem was reality. For three generations the farmers had lived in a system that provided cradle-to-the-grave security. It was neither efficient nor free, but it was safe. The Kazakh farmers were not about to become good homesteaders. Furthermore, they were discouraged by the fact that roads and power lines, such as they were, went to the old collectives, not to their new farms. There were no markets to speak of (in fact, the very idea of a market was unfamiliar to them); and there was no credit to allow the farmers to buy seed and equipment.

The Western experts were puzzled by the farmers' lack of initiative, but cautioned against any kind of a government program to help, including tax incentives to encourage foreign investment in rural areas. The minister was surprised to learn of the extensive government programs that protect and assist agriculture in the United States and Europe. It seemed to him that the experts were preaching what they did not practice at home. At the same time, the World Bank and IMF advisers insisted that the trade barriers that had protected the country's cottage textile industry be eliminated and three thousand people were left jobless. "When you make an omelet, you have to break some eggs," said one expert.

In order to seriously address poverty reduction in Kazakhstan, a way would have to be found to change the system over the long run. A recitation of free-market ideology will not do the job. And aid to the

Kazakh government will not change the system. The only way to do that is bit-by-bit and locality-by-locality using the skills, knowledge, and access to the world that only global corporations, such as Cargill, Nestle, Unilever, Bechtel, or Mitsubishi, can provide.

When all is said and done, in many parts of the world, it will not be governments that reduce poverty, nor will it be charities because there isn't enough charity money to make a difference; it will be business that does it and that will only occur if it is as an integral part of their profit-making activities, not a pro bono sideline. Only if poverty reduction is profitable will it be sustainable. And poverty won't be much reduced by lowering the cost of goods available to poor people.[11] A far stronger impact will be made through greater investment and more jobs. It will take the involvement of big business, global corporations that have the means and the reach to bring small local businesses into being, with the output of those smaller firms consequently being demanded by bigger, normally foreign firms. Of course, in most cases it is risk that stops big companies from delivering all of this all of the time. More on this in chapter 8.

## The Meaning of Development

The second reason that business involvement is so essential to poverty reduction relates to the nature of the system that breeds poverty, a system that must be changed if the poor are to flourish. Poverty is about more than income; it is a matter of power and being without it, not just now but generation after generation. Without basic change, no amount of talk about free markets and balanced budgets will make a difference. And corporations are superb engines of change.

So here we come to the meaning of the word *development*. Since the end of World War II it has been assumed that development was an economic process, naturally to be managed by economists. This erroneous assumption had the advantage of making it seem nonpolitical and therefore noncontroversial.[12] Who after all could be against "economic development"? It's like being against progress. The reality is that in much of the poor world—many countries in Latin America, Africa, Central and East Asia—development as poverty reduction means change and often radical change: land reform; access to markets and credit; access to political influence; a permanent and irreversible reallocation of power.

It is with such change that the individual gains the hope and the motivation that is a prerequisite for education. The fortunate go to school and work hard because they know that there is a ladder out there and that if they try they can climb that ladder and gain influence over their lives. The poor have no such confidence. There is no ladder. For them school seems irrelevant no matter how much money might be spent on schoolhouses, teachers, and textbooks. As a result of such despondency, children are not encouraged to go to school; many fail to attend at all or drop out early.

Needless to say, if development means change of this nature, then it is intensely controversial. In fact, its least significant aspect is economic; it is much more political, social, cultural, and psychological. It raises such questions as: Who is changing whom? For what purpose? In whose interests? At what speed? Does the status quo welcome change or will it fight it tooth and nail? And if there is to be a fight, can the change process be protected?

### Engines of Change

A number of years ago, one of the authors wanted to learn about the introduction of change. Together with a team of Harvard Business School students, he launched a research project in a rural province of Panama called Veraguas. There he and his team helped Bishop Marcos McGrath and his followers change the prevailing system.[13]

Veraguas was a remote province with a population of 150,000, located 150 miles west of Panama City. Like much of the rural world, its people had little sense of belonging to a nation. It was the seat of power of two or three families who owned most of the fertile land. It had languished in poverty since Columbus discovered it (he was the first Duke of Veraguas). The bishop, his priests, and their band of young laymen succeeded in introducing change, establishing some forty small cooperatives for purposes of increasing production and improving the peasants' access to credit and the market. Later a large, multiservice cooperative was introduced to the community along with a vocational training school, a radio station, a training center for cooperative leaders, and a large chicken factory.

The bishop's movement was an engine of change. Because of it, several thousand families moved from a system in which they had no ability to control their environment to one in which they had power. They owned some land. They had access to markets and thus the term "free market" had some meaning. They had access to credit, which gave them some financial power. They were motivated. For the first time they knew the value of education; there was indeed a ladder that with schooling a young person could climb and gain in power and influence. They built their own school and hired a teacher who taught what they believed needed to be taught—how to fix refrigerators. They were organized. They had leaders. When the leaders said boil the water, they boiled it, and dysentery was alleviated. Health, it turned out, was not as much a medical problem as it was a political and organizational one. In fact, experts who failed to understand the system within which Veraguas peasants lived were a menace. They made things worse. A seed specialist sent earlier by the government had told a subsistence farmer to plant tomatoes. He did and they flourished to such an extent that the land-owner on the hill decided to extend his fences to include the land that he previously thought worthless, thus worsening the farmers' plight.

The Veraguas movement reduced poverty. It introduced change. To those involved it was revolutionary change. Inevitably, the status quo retaliated. Two priests were killed. But to an outsider the change seemed modest, indeed. It was slow, difficult, and always tenuous. The government not only was no help; it was a major obstacle. Because of the canal, in those years Panama received more U.S. aid per capita than any other country. But if the aid reached Veraguas at all, it was in the form of National Guard troops or technical experts who had no under-standing of the system they were entering.

Observing what had occurred in Veraguas, a doctrine about the intro-duction of change emerged: the setting into which the change is to be introduced must be viewed as a whole, a circle of interrelated elements that are social, political, economic, cultural, physical, and psychological. An engine of change must be able to hit that circle on a wide arc, using

the solution of one problem—say, access to credit—to open the way to
solutions to other problems—health or education, for example.

A successful engine of change follows a sequence of action beginning
with *agitation*, meaning education about a precise need. (In Veraguas
the need was credit at a lower price than was charged by the village
*tienda* keeper.) When the need was met, a new confidence led to *motivation* and *organization*, the willingness and trust to join with others to
make change. Finally, there comes a *commitment* to continue the change
process.

An engine of change also has certain characteristics, starting with:

(i) *authority*—when the leader, the bishop or his agents,
    speaks, he must be listened to and believed;

(ii) *communication*—the ability to reach the most remote person
    that one is trying to affect;

(iii) *access to power*—the ability to protect the change process
    from the retaliation of the status quo; and

(iv) *competence*—that is, skills that vary as the change process
    proceeds.

At first, charisma might be important; then later, accounting or how
to fix a radio station becomes more of a priority. (In Veraguas it was
clear that the Panamanian government lacked virtually all of these characteristics. It was not to be trusted or believed; its agents had little
knowledge of or sympathy for the rural poor; it was beholden to the
status quo and therefore opposed to change; and its competence was
unrelated to the task.) So the presence of an engine of change with
these characteristics is a prerequisite to poverty reduction. Any injection
of resources that falls outside such an engine (e.g., the tomato seeds)
does not promote change; invariably it retards it.

As a further example, in the province next to Veraguas the Nestle
Company had started a dairy operation to produce powdered milk that
involved several thousand farmers. Its characteristics, the procedures it
followed, and the effects it achieved were similar to those of the bishop's
movement. There was, however, one important difference: it generated
profits. As we noted earlier, there isn't enough church, charity, or tax
money to introduce the change the world needs. That is why business
is so crucial.

Returning to Veraguas, if we consider the characteristics that made the bishop's project succeed there we can see that corporations have it in their power to be the world's most effective engines of change for the reduction of poverty. First, there is the competence they bring: skills, technology, access to global markets, and credit. The market does not work by itself. For the poor to benefit from the market mechanism, special efforts are required. For example, it's not enough to connect a rural village to the Internet; the villagers must know how to use that facility. Second, the corporation brings access to power. It can reach the levers of governmental power; it can get a road built or a power line strung. By motivating, organizing, and educating its people the corporation becomes an instrument for participation in government by those who before were excluded. With such power they can protect the change process from those who would destroy it. Third, these two capabilities give the corporation the authority and the ability to reach and be trusted by the most remote and dislocated of the poor. And finally, it has continuing will. It is not here today and gone tomorrow.

DaimlerChrysler was an engine of change in Brazil's poverty-stricken northeast. In 1992, having come under pressure from the Green Party in Germany, DaimlerBenz (as it was then known) started to look for ways to use more renewable natural fibers in its automobiles. (This was a time when, in the wake of the Rio Summit, many large, responsible, forward-thinking companies were striving to achieve what became known as greater eco-efficiency.) At the same time, the Brazilian government was demanding that companies with manufacturing facilities in the country increase the local content of what they produce. To address both problems, Joachim Zahn, the head of DaimlerBenz in Brazil at the time, arranged with a community development project in Belem called POEMA to construct a modern, high-tech factory that would make headrests and seats out of coconut fibers from locally grown trees. As of today some 5,200 people are employed by this project. For these formerly impoverished Brazilians, life has changed for the better. Their children are now in school and doing their homework, not dropping out. People have become more politically active. Health has improved. Although this operation will eventually turn a profit for DaimlerChrysler, it could not have happened without the help of the German and Brazilian governments.

For the last five years, the Shell Foundation has been working in Africa to support local enterprises that reduce poverty. In its March 2005 report, Kurt Hoffman, the foundation's director, wrote of the importance of connecting large MNCs to these enterprises. "Big companies possess a wide-ranging set of tangible assets that can be of huge value in the fight against poverty." He mentioned three categories of assets: first, the general knowledge of their people; second, their access to world markets; and finally, their "convening power": because of their track record, reputation, brand, political reach, and financial clout, when MNCs speak, people listen and respond. To engage MNCs in the work of poverty reduction the Report calls for "public-private partnerships" bringing together companies, NGOs, local government, and international development institutions.[14]

## MNC Involvement in the New International Consensus

There is, we detect, among relevant institutions and key policy-makers a growing acceptance of the insertion of MNCs into the broader "development" agenda. But practical implementation is proving problematic. NGOs remain skeptical; MNCs are not yet sure-footed; international financial institutions are increasingly conscious of their own limitations. One strong limitation is that there is no record of the previous contribution of MNCs to the reduction of global poverty. How much have they already done to ease the plight of the world's poor? For each additional unit of effort and investment by MNCs, what magnitude of improvement to livelihoods do they induce? We shall discuss these questions further in the following chapter. Much of the answer lies in the degree of "permission" big business has to fashion their business activities. Figure 6.2 illustrates this concept.

For most of the last several decades the world's MNCs have been exhorted to "do less" and to "do no harm." In effect, they were being pushed by "community" pressure to reduce their "footprint" and minimize their impact on the world. This push was driven by those advocating a pro-environment and pro–human rights agenda. Companies necessarily responded to community and, later, legislative pressure and improvements were achieved. In more recent times, MNCs are increas-

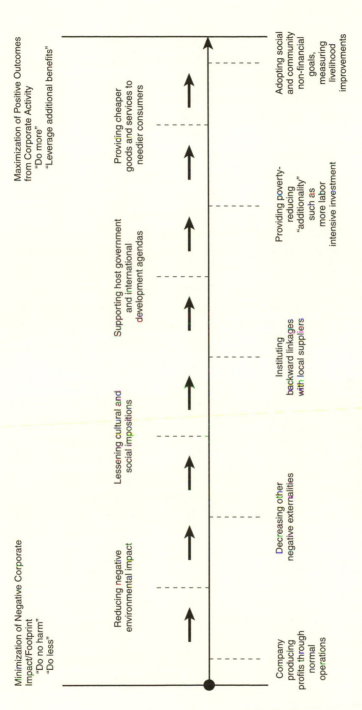

Figure 6.2. Trend in "permission" for big business activity.

ingly gaining a "license" to "do more" and to work toward maximizing
outcomes from their operations. This applies to social and community
projects, activities that achieve greater environmental effectiveness, and
strategies that reduce poverty through extensions of normal corporate
operations. This is evidenced by the gently growing rapprochement between NGOs and companies, the changing explicit organizational mission statements of companies adopting social objectives, and corporate
links to the international development agenda.

Some observers have begun to identify the growing momentum regarding the roles of MNCs in development and beyond the strict realm
of profit-producing operations. The *Financial Times* referred to this in
a series of articles in June 2004. "A fascinating new understanding has
begun to arise between two former sparring partners over the course of
only a few years. One of them is private enterprise: driven by profit but
always looking for new ideas and opportunities and with a deep interest
in conducting its business in a prosperous and predictable environment.
The other is the development world: horrified that much of the planet
remains so poor but chastened by decades of failed aid programs and
misguided experiments in social redistribution. Both groups have traditionally viewed each other with mistrust, if not overt hostility. Many in
the development world believed private industry had little interest in
social justice and limited relevance to governments' efforts to provide
basic services."[15]

MNCs want their markets to be safer, richer, more predictable. Development institutions want to make good on their goal of poverty reduction. But the latter are realizing that esoteric macroeconomic reform
is necessary but not sufficient and that old models of aid are unsustainable and ineffective. Observed the *Financial Times*:

> "A lot of developing country governments have spent the last 10
> years restructuring their public sectors: and suddenly are looking
> over the edge of the road," says Mark Malloch Brown, (then)
> head of the UN Development Programme. "What's missing is
> jobs and growth. There is no sign of an emerging tax base to sus-
> tain services in the future. Why not? There's a remarkably thin
> middle." The UNDP and others believe that multinationals can
> play a crucial role in fostering this "missing middle," the small

and medium enterprises, through support for local suppliers—with the added benefit that local people may show an interest in seeing them stick around. This coming together of communities has created an extraordinary opportunity. "There is a confluence of interests," says Nancy Birdsall, president of the Centre for Global Development. "It's a very exciting time: there is a grand convergence," agrees Joseph O'Keefe, from the International Finance Corporation."[16]

Measurements and best practice are not enough. Businesses have been measured on financial performance for centuries, but this does not mean that they are all able to maximize their financial value efficiently. There is no shortage of research findings, best practice reports, and management theories available to companies, but these are ineffectual if they are not accompanied by deep-rooted behavior change. This suggests that the mere measurement of social and environmental impact and dissemination of best practice will not by themselves lead to better outcomes for society and greater legitimacy for companies.

In fact, measurements and best practice can in some ways be inimical to innovation. Short-term pressure to meet targets and demonstrate best practice tends to work against companies' ability to find new solutions to problems.[17] It is increasingly being argued that the best contribution that companies can make to the social good is through innovation, and this will be killed if a standardized view of the "right way" to do CSR becomes embedded.[18]

As noted earlier, the final report of the March 2002 UN Conference on Financing for Development and the 2002 UNCTAD World Development Report both identified foreign direct investment as now being the largest single form of external finance for developing countries. The implication of this finding was that large multinational companies, the providers of the FDI, can make a greater contribution toward reducing poverty and improving economic governance in developing countries. A subtle shift is currently taking place—a shift in obligations, responsibilities, and imperatives for economic governance and poverty reduction—away from governments and international organizations to multinational companies and their strategic partners. This was witnessed again at the August 2002 World Summit on Sustainable

Development. But the new demands that are being placed upon multinational companies fall outside their areas of core competency and competitive advantage.

A key reason why this shift is occurring is because current models of development, and the extant international development architecture, are failing to bring about positive change that is sufficiently rapid and sustainable. According to Joseph O'Keefe:

> Development institutions and developing countries are beginning to recognise the basic structure of global development finance is probably not going to change. Public sector development assistance is between Dollars 50bn and Dollars 60bn; while the private sector offers between Dollars 200bn and Dollars 300bn in cross-border flows . . . (and at the same time) . . . business is waking up to the development agenda, recognizing it has a vested interest in doing things a different way and better.[19]

Despite their willingness to respond, multinational companies often are simply not well equipped to do so adequately or efficiently. This emerging and perceived shift in obligations and responsibilities is one of the reasons behind the proposal to establish the World Development Corporation. In the following section of the book we outline the different possibilities facing companies, suggest how they can do more on a sustainable, commercial basis, and set out the parameters of the proposed World Development Corporation.

# PART III

Global Poverty Reduction and the Role
of Big Business

# 7

# The Options for Business Contributions

We can safely assume that most owners of shares in multinational corporations agree with Milton Friedman that the corporation's sole responsibility is "to make maximum profits for stockholders" while obeying the law.[1] Although theoretically appealing in its simplicity, as we have noted this proposition ignores a number of questions that managers confront in the real world. For example: What makes up the full set of determinants of profit? If profit means more benefits than costs, how are these benefits and costs to be defined and by whom? What are community expectations? And how is the definition changing over time? Does the manager pursue profit in the short run or the long run?

Although governments might enact laws to answer some of these questions, the legislative process is often long, imperfect, and incomplete. And increasingly the expectations of society and of the nongovernmental organizations that have mobilized to represent society go well beyond what governments can or want to do. In fact, in many countries the government is perceived not to be part of the solution but part of the problem.

In a remarkable article that appeared in *The Economist* of May 26, 2005, Ian Davis, worldwide managing director of McKinsey and Company, addressed the Friedman approach directly.

> The problem with "the business of business is business" mindset is . . . that it can blind management to two important realities. The first is that social issues are not so much tangential to the business of business as fundamental to it. From a defensive point of view, companies that ignore public sentiment make themselves vulnerable to attack. But social pressures can also operate as early indicators of factors core to corporate profitability: for example, the regulation and public-policy environment in

which companies must operate; the appetite of consumers for certain goods above others; and the motivation (and willingness to be hired in the first place) of employees.

And echoing the communitarian ideology set out in chapter 2, Davis wrote: "Paradoxically, the language of shareholder value may hinder companies from maximizing shareholder value. . . . Practiced as an unthinking mantra, it can lead managers to focus excessively on improving the short-term performance of their business, neglecting important longer-term opportunities and issues."[2]

## The Challenge of Change

The history of big business since the beginning of the Industrial Revolution is filled with conflict over these questions: interest groups spark a change in community expectations concerning such matters as child labor, industrial safety, minimum wages, environmental pollution, and racial and gender discrimination. There is a period, often a long period, during which a battle rages and eventually a new consensus is reached and new laws emerge. Wise managers are quick to perceive and understand this change process early and to adjust their behavior accordingly. Changes in society's expectations of MNCs are a constant and common occurrence, forcing companies to change their behavior in order to protect their profits. Often this has meant incurring considerable expense, but not to change would have imperiled future profits. Indeed, some people are now questioning the sustainability of the entire Industrial Revolution, maintaining that it was breech-born, that it considered only gross benefits and not costs, and that a new, second industrial revolution is actually under way. They say that without completely undoing the existing framework for corporate activity, or at least radically changing it, an improvement in outcomes will be difficult. Most MNCs are ready to act, but do not want to misstep.

In the developing world of today, governments often lack the desire or the ability to secure within their borders the changes that the "international community" regards as important, changes, for example, in such areas as human rights, poverty, and environmental conditions.[3] So, if corporations abide by the legal parameters of local developing country governments, they might well violate the expectations of the outside world. Furthermore, when it comes to poverty reduction, an area in which the corporation is the critical agent, many host developing country governments are especially disinterested or ineffective.

As a consequence of this impasse, the most farsighted managers of MNCs today realize that they cannot wait for governments to shape the community consensus and legal framework to which they can then conform. They must act as best they can to do what needs to be done— for example, by reducing poverty—gathering whatever legitimacy they can scrounge from national governments, NGOs, the UN, and other international institutions. Those that move most adroitly will benefit, and in the longer run so will their shareholders.

Those companies that embrace change fastest tend to benefit more than those that lag behind. This has always been the case for large companies and their response to changing demands. In the words of Peter Drucker: "The biggest challenge for the large company—especially for the multinational—may be its social legitimacy."[4] It is clear that innovation for sustainable development, or for poverty reduction, or for eco-efficiency, is premised on the same necessity as innovation for a new technology. Three corporate leaders put it this way: "To preserve the freedom to innovate, corporations will have to include in their development processes an evaluation of a broader set of impacts, including the social, environmental, and economic impacts of their innovations, thereby keeping themselves aligned with public expectations."[5]

Much of the need for change within companies relates to corporate governance, which used to relate primarily to the formal accounting and fiduciary responsibilities of companies and the oversight of companies by regulators. Today this is beginning to also include other factors, such as the extent to which a corporation produces positive social change. MNC managers investing in developing countries know that their investment is viewed by different parties through different lenses. In particular, they know that a critical external eye will examine foreign investment to see whether it brings more benefits than costs to affected communities. Many potential investors see their investment in a developing country in the following perspective:

Demand for investment capital is increasing throughout both the developed and developing world. At the same time, governments and multilateral agencies are cutting back on aid. As barriers to the free flow of capital fall, policymakers have come to recognize that the quality of corporate governance is relevant to capital formation. They also realize that weak corporate governance systems, combined with corruption and cronyism:

- distort the efficient allocation of resources;
- undermine opportunities to compete on a level playing field;
- ultimately hinder investment and economic development.[6]

MNC managers are realizing that if their own corporate governance requirements and standards do not mesh with those of the host country's economy, or if a host economy has poor standards, they will not be able to attract optimally priced and conditioned capital. This is because socially responsible investors, including the world's biggest pension funds as well as financiers, are increasingly becoming more vigorous in their requirements for high standards of corporate governance on the part of those who receive their investments.

The challenge for large companies, therefore, is to consider the requirement to change not as an opportunity cost but as a necessary productive investment. It is a necessary acceptance of complexity. That such acceptance requires more of a subjective judgment than an objective decision does not make it less important or valid. And the MNCs that have already incorporated the principles of, say, sustainable development into their operations are now better placed to respond profitably to community pressure to do more in other fields such as poverty reduction. A growing number of companies are reaping the benefits from already having moved in this direction. IBM, for example, recently presented its first-ever corporate social responsibility report alongside its traditional annual accounts. IBM CEO Samuel J. Palmisano wrote a covering note that began:

All businesses today face a new reality, more important and lasting, in my opinion, than the advent of any game-changing technology or global market trend. . . . Businesses now operate in an environment in which long-standing societal concerns—in areas from diversity to equal opportunity, the environment, and work force policies—have been raised to the same level of public expectations as accounting practices and financial performance.[7]

Shell is another company that has come to the same realizations, as described in box 7.1.

Often it is crisis that brings about positive change in corporate behavior and practices.[8] Shell and Nike are two prime examples in which severe corporate trauma in the mid-1990s brought about radical change that has left the companies better off today. Their industry peers, of course, noticed what was happening and made similar changes, respective examples being British Petroleum and Levi Strauss, arguably being spared the worst of the traumatic transition. There is, of course, a catalytic and self-propelling effect at work here, as is evident in the example of the apparel industry's experience shown in figure 7.1.

### MNCs and Poverty Reduction

Alongside changes in corporate awareness over the last several years of the need to "do more and be better," world leaders have placed ever-increasing priority on poverty reduction—and terrorist attacks are sure to keep it high on the global agenda. Poverty is the seedbed of terrorism. It also causes political instability and economic uncertainty. It is bad for business. In addition, it is dehumanizing and offensive to the ideals that many communities and peoples cherish. So now, following calls from NGOs and the world's development agencies, the smarter MNCs are seriously thinking about how they can bring their capabilities more effectively to bear to help the poor while at the same time serving the long-run interests of their shareholders.

Despite ambiguities, reversals, and uncertainties, and often in the face of unstinting criticism (we need only look at the reasons behind the 1998 collapse of the UNDP's Global Sustainable Development Facility initiative), MNCs have committed themselves to doing more. Perhaps understandably, they already complain of what one executive termed "responsibility fatigue," but they also know that the pressure for them to do more will only grow, not recede.

Box 7.1

**Royal Dutch/Shell Group and Its Corporate Transition**

Shell drew the ire of the environmental movement when it came
to light in 1995 that the company planned to sink its Brent Spar
oil storage buoy in the North Atlantic Ocean. Greenpeace led the
charge. Also in the mid-1990s Shell got itself into trouble over its
arrangements with the government in Nigeria, where Shell has
operated since 1937, and the failure of its taxes to be spent effectively on public services for Nigerians. Former Chairman of the
Committee of Managing Directors of Shell, Philip Watts, described these events as simultaneously being catastrophes and also
blessings in disguise for Shell.

The events evoked a change in the company following the realization that it was out of touch with community expectations. The
company is now one of the world's best at pursuing broader sustainability and eco-efficiency objectives, and as a result the company is stronger and less susceptible to consumer boycott and other
risks. Shell executives later confirmed that job applications re-
bounded after having declined considerably before Shell took
steps to adjust its operations. A former Vice President for Sustainable Development at Shell, Tom Delfgauuw, said that responding
to these changes made Shell a much stronger company, "accelerated a great many needed corporate developments," and that
"transparency works, as does sharing dilemmas and difficult and
sensitive issues where (Shell was) not certain how to proceed."

SOURCE: Charles O. Holliday, Stephan Schmidheiny, and Philip Watts, *Walking
the Talk: The Business Case for Sustainable Development* (Sheffield, UK: Greenleaf
Publishing, 2002), pp. 19–21, 109, 136.

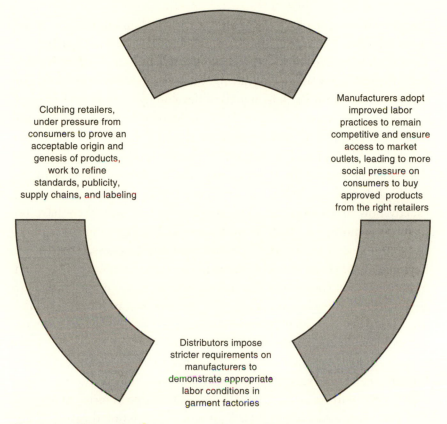

Clothing retailers, under pressure from consumers to prove an acceptable origin and genesis of products, work to refine standards, publicity, supply chains, and labeling

Manufacturers adopt improved labor practices to remain competitive and ensure access to market outlets, leading to more social pressure on consumers to buy approved products from the right retailers

Distributors impose stricter requirements on manufacturers to demonstrate appropriate labor conditions in garment factories

Figure 7.1. The cycle of pressure in the apparel industry.

Following are some preconditions for a successful MNC-led poverty-reduction mechanism.

- First, the mechanism must have a demonstrable and measurable positive impact, encouraging independent replication.
- Second, its activities need to be sustainable, which means profitable.
- Third, the mechanism and its activities should enhance corporate legitimacy, which means that it must carry the stamp of approval of the United Nations or another intergovernmental organization and a representative selection of NGOs.

Since no such mechanism exists, MNCs are in the invidious position of being urged to commit to a global and formalized effort to reduce poverty with no apparatus in place to legitimate their efforts or to make them effective. Neither is there any mechanism with the capacity and the mandate to investigate and document the profound effect MNCs have already had, and are still having, on global poverty reduction. For example, the World Bank in any given developing country will attempt to measure the impact of its projects on human development and increasingly link that to achievement of the Millennium Development Goals. It will also monitor changes in poverty levels over time. But no development institution is measuring the impact on poverty of an MNC. Likewise, an MNC in this same given country, while knowing exactly how many employees and suppliers it has, will likely have no idea of the multiplier effect its own operations are causing throughout the economy and the impact its investment and business activities are having on the lives of the poor. Indeed, the effects on poverty reduction of multinational corporations in this same country are not measured by anyone. Thus, there is no measurement, monitoring, or reporting of the improvements in poverty levels being delivered by, and attributable to, the world's multinational corporations.

To help advance their cause, MNCs need to convince their shareholders, their own executives, and staff that what they are doing makes sense, meets with society's expectations, is justifiable in terms of outputs and outcomes, and adds to their legitimacy. As we noted earlier, there are ongoing efforts, for example, by the Global Reporting Initiative, to value environmental improvements ("additionality") created by an MNC. It is difficult to do, but the tools of that trade are improving. Whether social value has been added or subtracted is even harder to calculate. The nebulous nature of these pursuits has tended to undermine the validity of so-called "triple-bottom-line" accounting that seeks to measure a company's social and environmental impact along with other, more conventional aspects of its performance. Nevertheless, the fact remains that ways to measure the human, nonfinancial impacts of corporate activity will continue to be refined and the resultant techniques will surely strengthen.

Pursuit of nonfinancial, often intangible, improvements is normally, and reasonably, justified as risk reduction (lowering such costs as insurance premiums and loan interest rates, for example). And today one way to look at the development challenges that corporations face is surely in terms of escalating risk. Thus, the inclusion of nonfinancial valuations into a company's decision-making, though difficult, has become compulsory even though it is a matter of managerial balance and judgment rather than quantitative analysis. MNCs, already pressed to go beyond conventional measurements of financial reporting to track social and environmental results, are now being called on, explicitly and implicitly, to provide a better indication of the impact of their activities on poverty in the countries in which they do business. But the response to this call is vague and uncertain, not least because they do not have the tools to do this.

Take the British American Tobacco Company (BAT) as an example. A long-established global company, it has been operating in Indonesia since 1908. It is large and profitable and no stranger to criticism from hoards of NGOs. Its managers in Indonesia can report on the number of employees they have, the number of farmers from whom they buy tobacco, and the number of acres of land under tobacco cultivation. But, as with other MNCs, BAT cannot report on the impact their activities have had over time on poverty levels and living standards. This is perhaps surprising since that impact is undoubtedly substantial and positive, especially during times in which Indonesian national poverty levels increased, as was the case in the 1960s during political upheaval and again in the late 1990s during the Asian financial crisis. There is no evaluation or reporting by BAT of the economic multiplier effect of company activities in the area of their footprint or of the degree to which poverty has consequently diminished at a localized or national level. Notably, in this example neither the Indonesian government nor the World Bank has calculated the impact on poverty levels by past and incoming FDI by MNCs.

Often stand-alone projects, especially start-up resource projects such as in mining, will be subjected to cost-benefit analyses, estimating the return on capital and the net present value of the investment. As these techniques have improved over time their scope has broadened so as to estimate economic values, as opposed to purely financial values. Thus, an investing company will consider the cost or benefit of a project from the perspective of different referent groups: the company (profits); the host government (taxes and other payments); and society (spillover effects, services, and wages). From these calculations it is possible to go

on to estimate the impact on poverty levels. Interestingly, even companies with large, ongoing operations are not in the habit of making these
calculations, despite the fact that they are often likely to produce results
that would significantly benefit corporate reputation.

The increasing pressure for MNCs to do more obscures the improvements in sustainable livelihoods that MNCs have already delivered. One wonders what impact MNCs have in fact had on poverty
reduction over the last century. What would be the level of wealth
of the world's six billion people today without the efficient resource
allocation decisions and technical and financial capacities and advances
of the world's large corporations over the last decades? Unfortunately,
it is impossible to know. The supporting data are simply not available.
Financial information from companies focuses on revenues and ex-
penses, assets and liabilities. Most international and national macroeconomic data deal with flows rather than stocks. The jury is even out
on the relationship between economic growth in developing countries
and foreign direct investment inflows. (The best evidence suggests that
they are probably mutually reinforcing.) What we do know is that economic growth, induced by many and varied drivers such as investments
in education (long-term) and investments in anticorruption initiatives
(short-term), is the best way to induce macro-level reductions in poverty. Most economic growth is delivered through growth in investment
as well as productivity gains, which, in turn, are often the result of
increasingly efficient investment, which is increasingly determined by
microeconomic factors. And wealth inequality, which has always been
around, is best reduced when the benefits of that economic growth are
optimally spread.

As we saw in chapter 5, the gap in the international architecture in
relation to tapping the resources of MNCs is readily apparent. We noted
that many international institutions are focused on poverty-reduction
issues and that some maintain guidelines and voluntary principles for
MNC corporate behavior. More recently, many of these intergovernmental organizations are pushing toward greater engagement with multinational corporations with an emphasis on advancing their role in poverty reduction in developing countries. But no universal mechanism
exists to facilitate the extension of MNC efforts, whether for:

    (i) collective advocacy on investment climate issues and recommendations for improvements;

    (ii) support for systems for calculating the poverty-reducing effects of MNC investment and business activity, globally and in individual countries; or

    (iii) expansion into arrangements that harness MNC skills and bestow greater legitimacy on activities explicitly aimed at reducing poverty.

To be sure, big companies are being exhorted to make available more goods and services at lower costs to the poor masses in developing countries.[9] This might reduce costs facing the poor and increase their consumption, but it represents more a new marketing strategy than a program to reduce poverty. For example, Coca-Cola has been marketing to the poor for a long time, but the impact of this on poverty is unclear. It should be recalled that most poor people believe their poverty is reduced much more by increases in income derived from employment and self-employment than through reduced costs of consumer goods.[10] This is an important point to recognize, and it is too often forgotten. Although vaccinations for children, improved maternal health care, and better roads help, jobs and direct income are the surest, most direct way to alleviate poverty. This is why the investment and flow-through effects of MNCs in poor economies are so important. For each investment that does not occur, the opportunity cost to poverty reduction is borne by those who can least afford it.

In poor countries MNCs play an important role in driving economic growth and encouraging domestic investment by smaller local businesses. MNC investments are normally highly efficient and scale is more readily achieved. They spread wealth through the economy by their wage payments, purchase contracts, and local distribution arrangements, as well as through tax payments that support public services by governments. In some countries, the taxes paid by MNCs amount to significant portions of government revenue.

With at least some of the battle regarding the relative weight and incidence of negative externalities caused by MNC operations having been won, largely through effective remedial action, attention is now turning, with greater confidence among civil society and international organizations, to extending the impact of MNCs in pursuit of a broader range of outcomes. Accordingly, it seems that MNCs are ready to be included in development-type programs and projects that reduce global poverty, which they feel will also add to their legitimacy and not undermine (but may, in fact, add to) their profits. This vision fits neatly with the prevailing view of many executives in MNCs, and development practitioners elsewhere, that much of what MNCs already do has profoundly positive implications for the lives of poor people. Remarked Peter Woicke, former executive vice president of the International Finance Corporation, in an address to corporate executives in October 2004: "Developing countries are the crossroads of corporate social responsibility for this generation, the place where all the major trends come together: population, poverty, health, water, energy, environment. Yet many of the institutions who should be at the crossroads working on these issues *have not figured out how to get there*" (italics added).[11] Our answer to this problem is the World Development Corporation, discussed in chapter 8.


## Options

There are various pioneering options available for businesses to consider if they decide to incorporate the objective of reducing poverty into their operations. Calculating the multiplier effect of a business on poverty reduction is one. The multiplier effect can, for example, be estimated in conjunction with a cost-benefit analysis of a new investment project. Or it might be done for an existing business based on the business's spending and flow-through effects on the host economy. It is common for global companies to monitor the value of their taxes and salaries paid within the footprint of their operation. These data are often used as a bargaining chip in dealings with host governments. In addition, however, big companies that have the data available have the ability to estimate the effect of their investments and transactions on the per capita wealth of the people in their communities. This can be compared against extant poverty thresholds in that country or territory and so an assessment can be made of the difference in poverty levels that is attributable to the business's presence.

Although company operations have long reduced poverty, the magnitude of the impact in poverty terms has not been systematically measured. Results have been measured mostly in terms of positive or negative return on capital. Where calculations reveal a positive result, however, as they will most of the time, poverty-reducing efforts should add considerable value to big companies in the form of lessened political risk, strengthened markets, cheaper or easier finance, and improved corporate reputation. This should increase profits as well as political support, the latter being especially important where the rule of law is fragile.

MNCs, major resource companies particularly, are becoming more proficient at helping host economies manage the payments that flow to them in the form of royalties, taxes, and the like. In the past, poor management of these flows has led to massive losses of national wealth, even increases in poverty levels, and sometimes destabilizing political consequences. This has carried large and direct costs for locally operating MNCs, both in terms of receipt of lower levels of government servicing and worsened corporate reputation. As a result, MNCs, including resource companies such as ExxonMobil, are working with host governments, NGOs, and development agencies such as the World Bank to establish dedicated accounting systems to manage the sometimes massive inflow to government treasuries of resource rents. The fund management systems that are established incorporate strong public accountability and transparency arrangements and help prevent the siphoning of funds by corrupt elements in government. These fund management systems can also help distribute the flow of funds more equitably among local, provincial, and national governments as well as produce intergenerational benefits through long-term investment programs. Examples of this sort of action are the savings funds recently established to support royalty payments by ExxonMobil in São Tomé e Principe and ConocoPhillips in East Timor.

If we return for a moment to the example of BAT in Indonesia, we can readily demonstrate how to align company activities with the ongoing development goal of reducing poverty. By taking a particular area of operations, say, in Central Java, the company can track its spending relatively easily. Using agreed multiplier coefficients on spending in the area, the company can estimate the full flow-through effect on the incomes in the local economy. Then, simply by taking a benchmark of local poverty levels and population at a given time, BAT would be able to estimate the number of people that its operations have lifted above various ex-ante poverty thresholds. These data can then be fed into broader poverty-reduction efforts being led by the development community for aggregation and extrapolation purposes.

In another example, Tata of India is preparing a $2 billion steel mill project in Bangladesh. Known for its high level of corporate responsibility, Tata is undertaking a host of impact assessments—environmental, social, and economic—in addition to its financial forecasting. Its strategies are designed to have as positive an effect as possible on the local community. Tata is planning to maximize the number of backward linkages to smaller local firms in the area as well as the local content used in its production processes. By taking a snapshot of the wealth levels in the area at the start of the project, then noting local poverty threshold benchmarks and collecting local income and wealth data over time, Tata should be able to monitor directly its effect on local poverty levels during the life of its project.

Project-based activities such as mining or infrastructure present a special problem because by definition they have a finite life; the project will come to an end in due course. What normally happens is that the company leaves a footprint—economic, social, and environmental—on the affected community, which then often suffers severe dislocation once the project has ended. In some cases the dislocation can be so serious as to essentially undermine all the economic benefits that have previously accrued. One mitigating strategy, therefore, is to devise plans to deal with the post-project period. Such a strategy should either aim to have sustainable related industries carry on after the core project has closed, something that can happen where subordinate businesses and industries have "clustered" successfully, or seek to reform the local economy ahead of project closure. An example of this sort of strategy is the post-project plan being conceived by Placer Dome of Canada at the Placer project in the highlands of Papua New Guinea. The mine has been operating for many years and is due to wind down over the next decade. Although the plan has a strong environmental focus, it aims to maximize the retained level of wealth and business activity in the local area. Together with the use of a development fund, this is another way of seeking to alleviate poverty on a sustainable basis.

As C. K. Prahalad has emphasized recently, poverty can also be lessened, and the changes measured, by providing better and cheaper products tailored for the poor. Companies such as Coca-Cola in China, Cemex in Mexico, Merck in Africa, and Hewlett-Packard in India have all made money by modifying their products, services, and marketing mix to turn poor people into customers. This can alleviate poverty and at the same time be sustainable, that is, profitable, and lower-priced consumer goods can lead to consumer surpluses and improved access to goods and services.

Nokia of Finland is another example of a company that has brought down costs, to increase accessibility to global communication networks. Small-scale entrepreneurs everywhere, in the developed and developing worlds alike, report that the ever-cheaper cost of sending a text message via e-mail to their suppliers and customers has enhanced considerably the efficiency of their businesses.

A key step to achieving some of the above is to remove company efforts aimed at poverty alleviation and social improvement from the province of the public affairs and corporate philanthropy departments and to ensure that those objectives become part of mainstream company operations. We have discussed at length what has caused companies to consider social effects: the pressure of NGOs, the need to retain their "license to operate," to ensure access to finance, and the fact that it is increasingly a good business proposition. But, as a rule, when a company is considering a new investment, or the continuation of an old one, effects on poverty are not considered because the decision-makers do not regard them as being their responsibility.

Another option is to improve the types of incentives facing MNCs when making investment decisions. Much of the inertia that is evident on the part of some large companies regarding poverty reduction can be traced to the incentives that are available to them to pursue social activities or achieve social benefits beyond legal obligations. In many cases, the incentives that can be identified by MNCs within a decision-making framework do not encourage them to invest. In Laos, for example, an MNC considering an investment in a food processing factory would recognize the low cost of labor and proximity to larger Thai markets, but the MNC has no incentive to include poverty reduction as a consideration when making the decision on its investment. Similarly, a large MNC that shifts its production facility from Uruguay to China in the wake of China's accession to the WTO has no incentive to include effects on poverty in its investment calculations and decisions, whether in Uruguay or China.

If, on the other hand, that same company wants to introduce improved environmental safeguards and machinery that reduce carbon emissions, there are incentives to which the company can attach value when it acts to provide a public good, in this case improved air quality. The incentive structure of the corporation, as we have seen, is based on the pursuit of profits. That profit objective is now more surely achieved by seeking to shore up legitimacy, that is, by not polluting. A company that reduces carbon emissions might be eligible to obtain a "carbon credit" which carries a positive financial value; it has an incentive to seek and measure improvements because it gets paid for doing so. The company also obtains intangible benefits arising from improved customer satisfaction and better relations with financiers. But what are the incentives for a company to align its operations directly and explicitly with poverty reduction? There is no clear and tangible benefit to tie business operations to the reduction of poverty. There is no thing we might term a "poverty credit," no dividend paid to a company for a unit of poverty reduction that results from an additional unit of investment.

For example, a given MNC might be considering an investment in a cement factory in one of two developing countries. Let us assume that all investment-related factors are equal in both countries. The only difference is that one country is poorer than the other. It is noteworthy that there is no incentive available that would encourage the company to invest in the poorer of the two countries, no "poverty credit," no formalized system of recognition, no cheaper finance. The shift of MNC investment from many developing countries to China in the last few years is worth examining in this respect. Often, this China-bound FDI has flowed from developing countries with higher levels of poverty than China. If incentives were to be made available to MNCs, then the impact on poverty reduction of the shift of FDI could be incorporated into the commercial decision-making process leading to net global improvements in extreme poverty levels. As a result of the Multi-Fiber

Agreement relating to textiles and apparel having expired at the end of 2004, there will probably be a transfer of investment from poorer developing countries to richer ones. In making a decision on the destination of their garment producing–related FDI, garment producers have no incentive to include the poverty levels (and potential for improvements in livelihoods) of their host economies into their commercial decision-making processes.

Of course, as we have noted, there are various mechanisms that do help MNCs invest in poor countries generally, and the CGD's index, to which we previously referred, helps to assess them. They consist of such things as double taxation agreements, bilateral investment treaties, political risk insurance, and independent dispute arbitration mechanisms. But these incentives are not tied explicitly to poverty reduction.

One can readily understand a company becoming confused when, with all the good intentions in the world, it wants to improve its performance as an agent of social advancement. Not only are there the competing legal and civil society demands to reconcile, but there is also the proliferation of business-related guidelines and voluntary codes and compacts. Some are legally binding, some are not. Those that are not legally binding might hold greater importance for one NGO, or one country, or one development organization, than for another. In a brief exchange with development officials at any given development or CSR-related conference, a CEO of a major corporation could be faced with questions about the declarations of the UN subcommission on human rights, or on the details of the Extractive Industry Transparency Initiative, the Sullivan Principles, the Equator Principles, SA8000, or whether his company's subsidiary in, for example, Suriname, was following all of these faithfully.

## Conclusion

There is clear and growing evidence that companies that have innovated to ensure good environmental safeguards, greater eco-efficiency, better organizational health and safety, and improved cultural and heritage protections have benefited from better political support and higher profits at lower risk. The same will become true of companies that play

an explicit role in poverty alleviation. In other words, gains are accruing
to those multinational companies that have consistently worked with
rather than against society's changing expectations.

In developing countries MNCs play an important role in promoting
economic growth because their investment is normally efficient and
substantial. They tend to spread wealth through wage payments and
purchase contracts and their tax payments enable the delivery of public
services. Now MNCs are being exhorted to pursue a broader range of
human development objectives as part of their core business operations. The task is for MNC leaders to organize a legitimate way to
achieve those desirable results while at the same time retaining commercial viability.

# 8

# A World Development Corporation

In this book we have set out two general propositions. The first relates to the nature of global poverty and the importance that has been attached to its reduction. The second concerns the legitimacy of the giant multinational corporations that are playing an increasingly important role in world governance. After a brief summary of these propositions we shall propose a new institution, the World Development Corporation. Its purpose is to reduce global poverty while invigorating MNC legitimacy.

## The Nature of Poverty

There are some countries in which government has played or is playing an effective role in poverty reduction: for example, China, India, and Vietnam today; and in the years since World War II, Japan, Taiwan, South Korea, and Singapore.[1] There are many more in which government either has been ineffective or has actually exacerbated poverty by sustaining the cancerous system that causes it. It is this second category that requires attention. Clearly, past efforts to help the poor by channeling money to these governments have not worked. Perhaps they even made matters worse. Foreign aid to the government of Panama, for example, did not help the poor of Veraguas. Aid to the government of Brazil might have benefited the poor in some places but did little in the northeast region of the country.

In such countries and regions, poverty is embedded in the political, economic, social, and cultural systems. To deal with it requires systemic change that opens the way to education, better health, political influence, and higher incomes. In chapter 6 we reviewed how an engine of change works and argued that MNCs in the regular course of their profit-making endeavors have the necessary characteristics to be an effective one. We offered some examples of corporations as change engines acting on their own and in concert with governments.

Even conceiving of the MNC as a vehicle to change systems in countries where the government is weak, or corrupt, is controversial, smacking of colonialism or forced globalization or worse. Though change is necessary and MNCs can effect it, many would ask: But can they be trusted? The answer, we believe, is yes, because if poverty is to be reduced there is no choice, and now MNCs have a vested interest in poverty levels, especially in light of the emerging global consensus surrounding developing-country poverty reduction. Great care must be taken to involve local partners, including healthy elements of local host governments, and to provide for monitoring by legitimate international organizations such as the United Nations and by effective organizations from the NGO community.

Furthermore, we believe that it is essential for MNCs to act collectively both to reduce the risk for any one corporation resulting from a single investment and to provide the range of capabilities that poverty reduction requires. Shell in Ethiopia is an example. A team of companies, rather than just Shell, is required to introduce solar-powered irrigation, and the whole effort is being carefully designed with local partners, including NGOs, under the sponsorship of the United Nations Development Programme.

## The Legitimacy of the Corporation

The traditional ideas from which corporations have derived their legitimacy are no longer adequate sources of management authority. These ideas emphasize the rights of property embodied in the corporation's shareholders, the efficiency of the market, the justice of competition, and the value of scientific specialization in generating new technology. As we argued in part 1, these ideas are becoming less reliable: shareholders do not "own" the company in any meaningful sense; competition to satisfy consumer desires in the marketplace does not necessarily meet the needs of the community; and scientific experts unaware of their effects on the whole can be a menace. World opinion, expressed in countless ways including the actions of thousands of NGOs, expects corporations to be mindful of community needs. This is, of course, an especially complex problem in countries in which government lacks either the desire or the ability to define and fulfill people's needs. In such countries—and there may be as many as sixty of them—the corporation in some ways becomes government, a role it is often unprepared or ill-equipped to assume. Nevertheless, MNCs need, in their own interest, a way to deal with this circumstance. Their legitimacy depends upon it.

Although the definition of community needs that MNCs should serve is controversial, few would argue that poverty reduction and all that goes with it—education, health, and political participation—is not such a need. Therefore, we propose that a new institution be created by a select group of global corporate leaders in cooperation with representative NGOs and the United Nations to address directly the problem of corporate involvement in poverty reduction.

## The WDC

The World Development Corporation will be a nonprofit corporation established under the auspices of the UN. It will harness the skills, capabilities, and resources of leading global corporations to reduce poverty and improve living standards in developing countries. It will work closely with existing international development agencies such as the World Bank, the International Finance Corporation, governmental foreign aid agencies, and civil society organizations (NGOs). The WDC will achieve its purpose by facilitating the creation of commercially viable business projects that combine maximum poverty alleviation with long-run sustainability.

The WDC will be organized and managed by representatives of a dozen or so multinational companies upon the invitation of the Secretary-General of the United Nations. They will be known as the Partners and will be the initial shareholders. Coming from many different regions of the world, they will represent a wide variety of capabilities and geographic interests.

The partners will name the WDC Board of Directors, which will include a representative chosen by the UN secretary-general, as well as representatives from NGOs. It is envisaged that the membership of the board will be composed of permanent and rotating directors drawn from shareholder companies. An advisory committee drawn from developing countries, civil society organizations, business, academe, and development agencies will complement the board. The partners may invite other reputable firms, perhaps to be known as Affiliates, to become financial and technical contributors to the WDC.

At the outset, the board will appoint a small secretariat and professional staff to commence and manage operations. While shareholders will provide the initial capital, it is expected that it will be augmented by funds from OECD governments and other development agencies.

The WDC will proceed experimentally, focusing on those countries or regions of countries that have received little or no foreign investment, that have been left behind by the processes of globalization. It will help partners and affiliates initiate commercial projects that promise a maximum impact on poverty. In consultation with local governmental and community leaders, it will identify project possibilities for the consideration of partners and affiliates. After project selection, it will assist in finding local partners to manage the project and coordinate assistance from development agencies. In all its activities the WDC will abide by the principles laid down in the Global Compact and seek to fulfill the Millennium Development Goals.

The WDC will advance project-by-project, gathering experience, and conducting research on what has worked and what has not. It will be very much a learning organization, and will thus become the foremost repository of knowledge about poverty reduction driven by commercial projects in the least developed countries of the world.

## Expected Achievements

### Poverty Reduction

The World Development Corporation is needed to fill the gap between the poverty-reducing intentions of international development agencies and the poor countries they are supposed to help. A review of the mission statements of these agencies—the UN Development Programme, the UN Conference on Trade and Development, the UN Industrial Development Organization, the World Bank, the International Finance Corporation, the Organization for Economic Cooperation and Development, the Inter-American and Asian development banks—(IDB) and (ADB)—and the European Bank for Reconstruction and Development (EBRD), just to name a few—will reveal that they are intent upon encouraging and facilitating investment to reduce poverty in poor areas of the world, often in those very countries, indeed, in which poverty has increased in recent years. Why have they failed? The answer is that there is a missing link between those agencies and the multinational corporations that have the capacity, the resources, and increasingly the will to do the investing. The WDC is that link.

Writing in *The Economist*, Jeffrey Sachs, special advisor to Kofi Annan, claims that "on anybody's list—the World Bank, Freedom House, Transparency International—a growing and significant number of African countries has the quality of leadership and governance to achieve economic development and to fight terrorism. But these countries lack the means."[2] He cites the dire lack of infrastructure: roads, electricity, health care, education. The need for infrastructure, however, is enormous. Where is the best place to start to ensure a systemic effect? Here is where the WDC comes in. If it existed, it could go to Ghana, for example, a country that has an admirable Poverty Reduction Strategy, and in cooperation with the local government, international institutions, NGOs, and relevant MNCs design a commercial project that would eventually be self-sustaining. This project would be the priority target for infrastructure development. Together with local partners, it would be owned by a consortium of WDC companies so that no single company would face too much risk. Oil companies regularly operate in a consortium fashion in difficult countries precisely for reasons of risk reduction.

The WDC will reduce poverty, especially in those regions of the world in which poverty has been most resilient, where individual companies are reluctant to invest alone, and in which traditional foreign assistance has been most disappointing. It can be expected that a wide range of benefits beyond raising incomes will flow from its projects: heightened motivation for education as children and parents perceive the possibility of a more rewarding future; improved health as nutrition improves and new social organization and community leadership emerge; and increased political participation as individuals gain power over their environment and begin to realize that they can change the system around them.

The WDC will implement the recommendations of the UN Commission on the Private Sector and Development (chapter 4) that called for the "unleashing" of small and medium enterprise in poor countries. The McKinsey Global Institute (MGI) has found that this unleashing depends on increasing the productivity of local enterprise, which is greatly enhanced by association with world-class business organizations.[3] Not only could the WDC facilitate such connections, it could also bring pressure to bear upon local governments to remove some of the barriers to competition that the MGI found so prevalent and counterproductive in the poor world. One is reminded of the success of Technoserve, a business-sponsored NGO, in attacking rural poverty in Latin America and Africa. It has organized projects in several countries, enabling Starbucks and Procter & Gamble, for example, to improve the productivity, quality, and profitability of thousands of small-scale coffee growers. The UNDP business partnership program mentioned in chapter 4 is another example of what the WDC could do more practically.

## Benefits to MNCs

The WDC will bring many benefits to its partners and affiliates. It will enhance their legitimacy as they prove their effectiveness in meeting community needs. It will provide companies that have huge, long-term investments in poor countries a way of safeguarding their investment against political instability. It is a vehicle through which local suppliers and markets can be developed. Finally, the WDC offers companies a collective approach to development that both lowers risk and increases the chances of success.

The research activities of the WDC will for the first time provide data on how MNCs can best contribute to improved economic development and governance, and lowered poverty, in developing countries. There are many important questions to which we have no answers today, among them:

- How, in fact, are MNCs responding to the mounting demands that they lead in improving economic governance in developing countries? (In writing this book we were surprised by how little is known about this.)

- How well equipped to lead do MNCs feel they are? What are their deficiencies?
- What are their true views on "corporate social responsibility" initiatives? Do shallow efforts of corporations to be "socially responsible" actually result in better economic governance and reduced poverty, or are they largely a veil to appease certain observers, another form of tax?
- What internal programs or projects have MNCs undertaken to try to improve economic governance and what has been the outcome?
- What could governments do to help MNCs in this area?

Most MNC managers with whom we have spoken are interested in the WDC idea. Any concerns they have are in relation to two factors. First, they fear that NGOs, already mistrustful of big corporations, would oppose what might appear to them to be a global monster. Second, they also wonder about returns to shareholders. NGOs acknowledge that poverty reduction requires investment by business in those territories where it is not invested. On the other hand, under the banner of antiglobalization, they oppose such investment. Stalemate has been the result.

Enlightened MNC managers have time and again pronounced their commitment to "sustainable development" and poverty reduction as being in the long-run interest of their shareholders. Therefore they should have no reason not to favor the WDC, since it will be the most efficient way of doing that to which they are already committed.

Perhaps NGO and MNC fears would be allayed if the initiative to establish the WDC were taken in concert with a group of NGOs that would invite corporate participation along the lines we have described.

## Practical Steps toward Implementation

Although we have found solid interest in the proposed World Development Corporation among people in companies, NGOs, government, and international organizations, there are many fears that must be dealt with if the WDC is to become a reality.

"It sounds awfully big," said one NGO official, "sort of like another Bretton Woods-type institution, which, of course, it's not. But it might be wise to start small and try to get in under the radar so to speak."

An experienced official at a multinational pharmaceutical company said: "It's an interesting idea, but I see two problems: the mistrust of antiglobalizers would be inflamed by the suggestion that an all-powerful world corporation would be created, and it's pretty far removed from the purpose of the company to create shareholder value."

A UN official said: "The politics are against you: anything new threatens what's old. Foreign aid agencies, the World Bank, and the rest fear that the WDC would detract from them. It wouldn't, of course. In fact, it would enable them to do their job better, but they're jittery as it is. They're also nervous about getting too close to business."

The same point was picked up by a thoughtful NGO official: "It's a dilemma. We know that poverty reduction requires MNC investment. At the same time we are wary of getting too close to business. We don't want to be tainted and NGOs watch each other like hawks on this. There's a lot of competition among us, and jealousy."

Finally, a spokesperson from a large MNC said: "Look, it's a great idea and I understand that UN sponsorship is necessary for legitimacy, but, to many businesspeople the UN is a huge bureaucracy not known for its efficiency. Then also the collective approach is kind of a two-edged sword. I can see that by acting together on WDC projects, companies would not only be more effective but would also minimize their risk. On the other hand, many companies are not entirely comfortable cooperating with one another. They are built to compete and if there is credit to be had, they each want it."

## Conclusion

In this book we have argued that the legitimacy of the world's global giants is in question. The old ideas in which their managers have rooted their authority are insufficient to meet global expectations. The corporation as the principal driver of globalization is now expected to pay greater heed to the needs of the communities that it affects, among which is the alleviation of poverty in much of the world. Although it has the skills and capabilities to address this need far more effectively than it has in the past, the corporation lacks the legitimacy to do so. This lack of legitimacy has several sources: first, the corporation is bound to serve its shareholders or else it won't survive; second, the intervention required to reduce poverty often entails the introduction of change that in the context of the poor country is perceived as radical and threatening to the status quo; and finally, the MNC has a questionable right to introduce radical change. There is thus a paradox. The corporation, in order to revive its legitimacy, is expected to do what in many ways is illegitimate. So it needs help. Much is at stake, because in a larger sense the success of MNCs and the revival of their legitimacy is crucial not only to poverty reduction but generally to a healthy world economy.

The remedy is to equip the corporation with the legitimacy that can be bestowed by the United Nations, NGOs, and the communities it affects, and also to provide it with sufficient public resources to enable it to serve community needs, that is, reduce poverty, without threatening its survival as a profit-making institution. This is what we suggest a World Development Corporation could do. Its creation would be a precarious task. It naturally arouses suspicion on all sides. But if there is no other way to do what needs to be done, surely it is worth a try. We believe that the poor will cheer its arrival.

# Notes

## Chapter 1
## Introduction

1. Stephen J. Korbin, "Multinational Corporations, the Protest Movement, and the Future of Global Governance," in Alfred Chandler and Bruce Mazlish, eds., *Leviathans: Multinational Corporations and the New Global History* (Cambridge: Cambridge University Press, 2005), p. 219.

2. Pierre Teilhard de Chardin, *The Future of Man*, translated from the French by Norman Denny (New York: Harper and Row, 1964), pp. 132, 228–229, 244, and 293.

3. See, e.g., John Braithwaite and Peter Drahos, *Global Business Regulation* (Cambridge: Cambridge University Press, 2000), pp. 27, 218, and elsewhere. Also, Peter Waldman, "Washington's Tilt to Business Stirs a Backlash in Indonesia," *Wall Street Journal*, February 11, 2004, p. 1.

4. *Foreign Policy*, March/April 2004, p. 54.

5. Brian Roach, "A Primer on Multinational Corporations," in Chandler and Mazlish, *Leviathans*, p. 35.

6. McKinsey Global Institute, *New Horizons: Multinational Company Investment in Developing Countries*, Washington, D.C., October 2003, Executive Summary.

7. Roach, "A Primer," p. 19: Chapter 11 of the North American Free Trade Agreement (NAFTA), for example, states that the governments of Canada, Mexico, and the United States cannot "take a measure tantamount to nationalization or expropriation" of a foreign investor without sufficient compensation. As of 2001 there were 17 cases in which corporations had used Chapter 11 to claim compensation for losses due to environmental regulation (p. 36).

8. Ibid., p. 30.

9. The generally accepted definition of FDI is from the Organization for Economic Cooperation and Development. Loosely, the OECD defines FDI as capital from abroad that is invested directly into a new or existing business in a foreign country and that the foreign stake in that enterprise, which is subject to foreign control, must equal at least 10 percent of total equity. FDI can meet this definition if invested in either a public or private company as long as the equity stake is at least 10 percent. Thus, FDI is distinct from foreign portfolio invest-

ment, which is normally invested in equities listed on a stock exchange at a rate, by definition, of less than 10 percent of total equity of that enterprise.

10. Sarah Anderson and John Cavanaugh, "Top 200: The Rise of Corporate Global Power," in Roach, "A Primer."

11. Medard Gabel and Henry Bruner, *Globalinc: An Atlas of the Multinational Corporation* (New York: New Press, 2003), p. 2.

12. Roach, "A Primer," p. 26.

13. Ibid., p. 28.

14. Andrew Walter, "NGOs, Business and International Investment: the Multilateral Agreement on Investment, Seattle, and Beyond," *Global Governance* 7 (January–March, 2001): 51.

15. Raymond Vernon, "Rogue Elephant in the Forest: An Appraisal of Transatlantic Relations," *Foreign Affairs* 51 (April 1973). See also Vernon, *Sovereignty at Bay: The Multinational Spread of U.S. Enterprise* (New York: Basic Books, 1971).

16. From www.thecorporation.com, p. 3.

17. Gabel and Bruner, *Globalinc*, p. 2.

18. World Bank, *World Development Indicators 2004* (Washington, D.C.: World Bank), April 2004.

19. Ibid.

20. Joseph E. Stiglitz, *Globalization and Its Discontents* (New York: Norton, 2002), p. 5.

21. Kofi A. Annan, *We the Peoples: The Role of the United Nations in the 21st Century* (New York: United Nations, 2000), p. 6.

22. International Finance Corporation, *Sustainable Investment*, Washington D.C., 2004, p. 1.

23. P. J. Simmons, "Learning to Live with NGOs," *Foreign Policy* 112 (Fall 1998): 82ff.

24. John Gerard Ruggie, "Taking Embedded Liberalism Global," in David Held and Mathias Koenig-Archibugi, *Taming Globalization: Frontiers of Governance* (Cambridge, UK: Polity Press 2003), p. 146.

25. Roach, "The Primer," p. 40.

## Chapter 2
### The Legitimacy of Business

1. Much of this chapter and the next are taken from George C. Lodge, *The Legitimacy of Business*, a paper written for the Philosophy of Management Conference, St. Anne's College, Oxford, July 2004.

2. See Antoine L. Destutt de Tracy, *Elements d'Ideologie*, 2d ed. (Brussels: A. Wahlen, 1826); Max Weber, *The Protestant Ethic and the Spirit of Capitalism*, trans. Talcott Parsons (London: Allen and Unwin, 1930); Karl Mannheim, *Ideology and Utopia* (New York: Harcourt Brace, 1953); and George C. Lodge, *The New American Ideology* (New York: Alfred A. Knopf, 1975), chap. 1, among others. See also the *Oxford English Dictionary*: "The science of ideas; . . ."

3. Adolf A. Berle and Gardiner C. Means, *The Modern Corporation and Private Property* (New York: Harcourt, Brace & World, 1967), pp. vii–viii. See also A. V. Dicey, *Law and Public Opinion in England* (London: Macmillan, 1952); and Alfred D. Chandler, Jr., *The Visible Hand: The Managerial Revolution in American Business* (Cambridge, MA: Harvard University Press, 1977), pp. 484, 498–500.

4. See the Gallup International Survey of 60,000 leaders in 50 countries commissioned by the World Economic Forum and described in a WEF press release issued in Geneva, Switzerland on January 12, 2005.

5. George C. Lodge, "Business and the Changing Society," *Harvard Business Review* (March–April 1974): 59–72.

6. Samuel Huntington, *American Politics: The Promise of Disharmony* (Cambridge, MA: Harvard University Press, 1981), p. 63.

7. We do not mean to suggest that Smith preached laissez-faire; he was after all embedded in a system in which government regulation was plentiful and for the most part accepted. Nevertheless, he did write in *The Wealth of Nations*: "It is not from the benevolence of the butcher, the brewer, or the baker that we expect our dinner, but from their regard for their own interest."

8. Ibid., p. 39.

9. George Wehrfritz and Ron Moreau, "A New Kind of Company," *Newsweek International*, June 5, 2005, pp. 10–12.

10. In a recent study, Luscious Bacchus of Harvard Law School found that between 1996 and 2002 there were fewer than two attempts each year to vote out directors of American firms with over $200 million in sales (*The Economist*, May 1, 2004, p. 13).

11. Jennifer Rheingold and Fred Jazzperson, "Executive Pay," *Business Week*, April 17, 2000, cited in Neva R. Goodwin, "The Social Impact of Multinational Corporations: An Outline of the Issues with a Focus on Workers," in Chandler and Mazlish, *Leviathans*, p. 153.

12. Goodwin, "Social Impact," p. 162.

13. See Braithwaite and Drahos, *Global Business Regulation*, p. 218 and elsewhere.

14. See Hernando de Soto's work on property rights for the poor.

15. Clive Crook, "The Good Company: A Survey of Corporate Social Responsibility," *The Economist*, January 22–28, 2005, pp. 3, 4, 10.

16. "A Survey of America," *The Economist*, November 8, 2003, p. 19.

17. Geoffrey M. Hodgson, *How Economics Forgot History: The Problem of Historical Specificity in Social Science* (London and New York: Routledge, 2001), pp. 30, 31, 252, 253.

18. Thomas K. McCraw, "The Trouble with Adam Smith," *American Scholar* 61 (1992): 371.

19. Foreword to David Henderson, *Misguided Virtue: False Notions of Corporate Responsibility* (London: Institute of Economic Affairs, 2001), p. 8.

20. Foreword to *Responsible Business*, published by the *Financial Times* of London, quoted in Henderson, ibid., p. 125.

21. Quoted in Henderson, *Misguided Virtue*, p. 24.

22. Milton Friedman, *Capitalism and Freedom* (Chicago: Chicago University Press, 1982), p. 133.

23. Charles O. Holliday, Jr., Stephan Schmidheiny, and Philip Watts, *Walking the Talk: The Business Case for Sustainable Development* (Sheffield, UK: Greenleaf Publishing, 2002), pp. 242–244, 255.

24. Ibid., pp. 242–244, 255.


## Chapter 3
### NGOs and the Attack: Critics, Watchdogs, and Collaborators

1. The term "vigilante," which is particularly appropriate here, we took from Kimberly Ann Elliott and Richard B. Freeman, "White Hats or Don Quixote? Human Rights Vigilantes in the Global Economy," Working Paper 8102, National Bureau of Economic Research, 2001, Cambridge, MA.

2. P. J. Simmons and Chantal de Jonge Oudrant, eds., *Managing Global Issues: Lessons Learned* (Washington, D.C.: Carnegie Endowment for International Peace, 2001), p. 717.

3. Michael Edwards, *Civil Society* (Cambridge, UK: Polity Press, 2004), p. 23.

4. Ibid., pp. 21–22.

5. Ibid., p. 22.

6. Simmons, "Learning to Live with NGOs," pp. 82–96.

7. Marc A. Thiessen, "When Worlds Collide," *Foreign Policy*, March/April 2001, p. 64.

8. See Elliott and Freeman, "White Hats or Don Quixote's?"

9. Ruggie, "Taking Embedded Liberalism Global."

10. Jim Bendell and David F. Murphy, *Partners in Time? Business, NGOs and Sustainable Development* (Geneva: UNRISD, 1999), UNRISD synopsis.

11. Ibid.

12. *The Economist*, August 9, 2003, p. 55.

13. Walter, "NGOs, Business and International Investment."

14. Ibid.

15. Refer to ICC press release of June 9, 2004.

16. Ruggie, "Taking Embedded Liberalism Global," pp. 104–105.

17. Stephen Fidler, "Who's Minding the Bank?" *Foreign Policy* 126 (September/October 2001): 40–50.

18. Ibid., p. 46.

19. Ibid.

20. Ibid., p. 49.

21. *Foreign Policy Magazine*, September/October 2004, p. 50.

22. The mission statement of CorpWatch, taken from its Website, is: "CorpWatch counters corporate-led globalization through education, network-building and activism. We work to foster democratic control over corporations by building grassroots globalization, a diverse movement for human rights and dignity, labor rights and environmental justice."

23. Corpwatch, Press Release, June 14, 2004.

24. Ibid.

25. From www.thecorporation.com.

26. Quoted in Charles O. Holliday et al., *Walking the Talk*, p. 150.

27. Ibid., p. 137.

28. James K. Brown, "Corporate Soul-Searching: The Power of Mission Statements," *Across the Board* 21 (March 1984): 44–52.

29. This was taken from the Global Reporting Initiative Website.

30. "SRI Sets Out Corporate Disclosure Guidelines," in *Environmental Finance*, October 8, 2004, reproduced by the World Business Council for Sustainable Development.

31. This was drawn from the BSR Website, 2004.

32. Ibid.

33. The Conference, held December 12 to 14, 2004, and entitled "Eradicating Poverty Through Profit: Making Business Work for the Poor," was intended to build on the understanding of private-sector contributions to development and the notion that business can "do good and do well" at the same time.

*Chapter 4*
*The Corporate Response*

1. "Power and Responsibilities: The Role of Corporations in Human Progress," speech by Lord Browne, Chairman of BP, delivered to the Princeton Environmental Institute as the 2004 Tallinn Environmental Lecture, October 4, 2004.

2. Friedman, *Capitalism and Freedom*, p. 133.

3. KPMG Canada, KPMG Ethics Survey 2000—Managing for Ethical Practice, Canada, 2000.

4. In 2004, the IFC's Operational Strategy Group prepared an overview on the business case for sustainability. It reviewed various sources, including internal corporate assessments as well as academic research, to determine whether corporate investment in activities related to environmental improvements, strengthened corporate governance, and widened social objectives helped the profitability of corporations. The overview found that, while evidence was patchy and still being gathered, there was a strong basis to assert that profit was enhanced by such efforts. Improvements came in the "hard" form of both increased revenues and lessened costs, and in the "soft" form of improved brand reputation and lower corporate and political risk.

5. Henderson, *Misguided Virtue*, p. 28.

6. Danish Institute for Human Rights, "Strengthening Implementation of Corporate Social Responsibility in Global Supply Chains," World Bank Group, October 2003.

7. Henderson, *Misguided Virtue*, pp. 12–15.

8. World Bank Institute seminar entitled "Development and Corporate Responsibility: A New Challenge for Latin America," Washington, D.C., August 2, 2004.

9. Political and Economic Consulting, "Race to the Top: Attracting and Enabling Global Sustainable Business—Business Survey Report," World Bank Group, October 2003, pp. 2–5.

10. IFC, *Sustainable Investment*, pp. 4–5.

11. Ibid.

12. Adelle Blackett, Symposium: "Globalization, Accountability, and the Future of Administrative Law: Global Governance, Legal Pluralism and the Decentered State: A Labor Law Critique of Codes of Corporate Conduct," *Indiana Journal of Global Legal Studies* (Spring 2001): 11.

13. Ibid., p. 13.

14. Gary Gereffi, Ronie Garcia-Johnson, and Erika Sasser, "The NGO-Industrial Complex," *Foreign Policy* 125 (July–August 2001): 56–57, 63. See also Ruggie, "Taking Embedded Liberalism Global," pp. 108–116.

15. "The Role of Public Policies in Promoting CSR," submitted by the German Federal Ministry for Economic Cooperation and Development to the 2003 European Conference on Corporate Social Responsibility.

16. Elliott and Freeman, "White Hats or Don Quixote?" p. 26.

17. ISO Advisory Group on Social Responsibility, Working Report on Social Responsibility, unpublished paper, April 2004.

18. Simmons, "Learning to Live with NGOs," p. 91.

19. Interview with Sirkka Korpela, Head of UNDP, March 31, 2004.

20. As an example, in "The Role of Public Policies in Promoting CSR," the Dutch submission to the 2003 European Conference on Corporate Social Responsibility, Roel Nieuwenkam of the Ministry of Economic Affairs noted that in the two years from 2001 to 2003 the percentage of Dutch companies undertaking a form of CSR rose from 20 percent to 72 percent.

21. The Institute of Social and Ethical Accountability, Press Release, September 20, 2004.

22. *Financial Times*, June 24, 2004, p. 3.

23. Ibid.

24. Drawn from "The Role of Public Policies in Promoting CSR," the submission by the Dutch Ministry of Economic Affairs to the 2003 European Conference on Corporate Social Responsibility.

25. Ibid.

26. From the Business Overview section of the Conversations-with-Disbelievers Website, at www.conversations-with-disbelievers.net/site/.

27. Ibid.

28. The ICC's 35th biennial World Congress was held in Marrakech in June 2004. The Congress adopted the theme of "Standing up for the World Economy" in a pronounced defense of the merits of globalization, while acknowledging that more needs to be done, including by global business, to ensure better and more equitable distribution of its benefits, especially in the developing world.

29. "Power and Responsibilities: The Role of Corporations in Human Progress," speech by Lord Browne, chairman of BP, delivered to the Princeton Environmental Institute as the 2004 Taplin Environmental Lecture, October 4, 2004.

## Chapter 5
### International Development Architecture

1. The World Bank's corporate mission statement is "Our dream is a world free of poverty."

2. World Bank's Poverty Reduction Strategy Sourcebook.

3. Deepa Narayan et al., "Voices of the Poor" (Washington, D.C., and Oxford: World Bank, Oxford University Press, 2000). The survey indicated that the poor felt that employment or self-employment was the most effective way to alleviate poverty, well ahead of, for example, increased thrift on their part, more access to credit, increased consumer surplus, or more certain title to agricultural land.

4. From www.worldbank.org.

5. The Strengthening Grassroots Business Organizations Initiative (SGBI) is designed to help a "new class of organization," socially driven businesses that are profit-oriented but with a social mission. The means of precisely defining these objectives are not concluded. The SGBI has commenced work with a number of pilot projects in various countries. Some examples include a bee-keeping project in Kenya (which was a recipient of the 2004 International Chamber of Commerce World Business Award) and an agricultural processing firm that buys organic produce from Bolivian farmers.

6. This was taken from the introductory note on the IFC's Strengthening Grassroots Business Organization Initiative, IFC, 2004.

7. Along with its work with the developed countries, OECD also gives much attention to the issues and challenges facing developing countries, 70 of which have become signatories to the OECD as nonmembers. As part of its work with nonmember countries, the OECD convenes the annual OECD Global Forum on International Investment, which examines with developing countries some of the issues related to attracting and extracting maximum advantage from foreign direct investment. The first Global Forum for International Investment was held in Mexico in 2001. The 2004 meeting was held in October in India.

8. OECD, "Foreign Direct Investment for Development: Maximising Benefits, Minimising Costs," Paris, 2002.

9. Ibid.

10. For example, the "Financing Development Colloquium" held on the Gold Coast, Australia, in August 2004.

11. Business Responsibility for Sustainable Development project description at www.unrisd.org.

12. There were originally nine principles covering human rights, environment, and labor standards. The tenth principle, on anticorruption, was added in 2004.

13. The UNDP commissioned a report by the International Business Leaders Forum in 2003, "Business and the Millennium Development Goals," as a "framework for action" on how business can work with governments, civil

society, and international agencies to help achieve the Millennium Development Goals.

14. The objective of the 2004 Global Compact Leaders Summit was to "harness the potential of markets and business leadership through shared values (the Global Compact's principles) and collective action so that global markets can be made to work for all.

15. Washington International Business Report, October 2004, pp. 1, 3.

16. Ibid.

17. This was taken from the preliminary report on the Global Compact Leaders Summit, July 2, 2004, p. 2.

18. Ibid., p. 1.

19. Press Release: International Chamber of Commerce, June 9, 2004.

20. "Growing Sustainable Business for Poverty Reduction," a paper published in 2004 by The Global Compact and the UNDP, p. 1.

21. Ibid.

22. "Supporting SME Entrepreneurship for Sustainable Development," UNDP Working Document, February 2004, p. 28.

23. The Commission was convened in July 2003 and released its report, "Unleashing Entrepreneurship: Making Business Work for the Poor," in March 2004. The Commission's report sought to highlight ways in which development objectives can be better met through leveraging development outcomes from additional private-sector growth and activities. The report is further referred to below.

24. C. K. Prahalad, *The Fortune at the Bottom of the Pyramid: Eradicating Poverty Through Profits*, Upper Saddle River, NJ: Wharton School Publishing, 2004.

25. "Unleashing Entrepreneurship: Making Business Work for the Poor," United Nations Development Programme, Commission on the Private Sector and Development, 2004, p. 41.

26. Canada, France, Germany, Italy, Japan, Russia, the United Kingdom, and the United States.

27. UN Press Release of June 10, 2004, on the G8 meeting. The Group of Eight referred to the work of the Commission on the Private Sector and Development in rather general terms. The G8 endorsed the general recommendations of the Commission, stating: "The UN Commission ... has stressed that poverty alleviation requires a strong private sector. It is the source of growth, jobs and opportunities for the poor." The G8's recommendations, however, centered more on improving access to microfinance, the development of SMEs and informal sector businesses, improvement of developing country business regulatory environments, and the lessening of costs associated with

remittance homeward of income earned in rich countries by poor country workers.

28. UNCTAD, "Linking International Trade with Poverty Reduction," The Least Developed Countries Report, 2004.

29. UNIDO's corporate mission statement is: "Fighting Poverty and Marginalization Through Sustainable Industrial Development."

30. UNIDO, *Operationalizing UNIDO's Corporate Strategy: Services and Priorities for the Medium Term, 2004–2007* (Vienna: UNIDO), p. iii.

31. Ibid.

32. "The Role of Public Policies in Promoting CSR," submitted to the 2003 European Conference on Corporate Social Responsibility by the Dutch Ministry of Economic Affairs, Conference Booklet, p. 30.

33. The conference was held in Venice, Italy, on November 14, 2003.

34. "Energy and Environment for Sustainable Development," UNDP working power-point document, 2004, p. 55.

35. Ibid., p. 62.

36. "The Role of Public Policies in Promoting CSR," submitted to the 2003 European Conference on Corporate Social Responsibility by the French Ministry of Social Affairs, Labor and Solidarity.

37. See Holliday et al., *Walking the Talk.*


## Chapter 6
### The Emerging International Consensus

1. "More Aid? Sounds Great but Wait . . . ," Speech to the World Economic Forum, 2002, quoted in Judy Shelton, *Wall Street Journal*, February 15, 2002.

2. Colin Bradford and Johannes F. Linn, "Global Economic Governance at a Crossroads: Replacing the G-7 with the G-20," Policy Brief #131 (Washington, D.C.: Brookings Institution, April 2004), p. 2.

3. "Timor-Leste—Poverty in a New Nation: Analysis for Action" (Washington, D.C.: World Bank, May 2003), p. 23.

4. The actual thresholds are closer to US$1.10 and US$2.15, respectively.

5. World Development Indicators 2004, World Bank, April 2004.

6. World Bank News Release No:2004/309/S, April 23, 2004.

7. Global Monitoring Report 2004: Policies and Actions for Achieving the Millennium Development Goals and Related Outcomes (Washington, D.C.: World Bank, 2004).

8. Ibid.

9. Tim Hartford and Michael Klein, "The Market for Aid Understanding," *Public Policy Journal*, published by the World Bank, Washington, D.C., June 2005, p. 2.

10. See Nicolas van der Walle, "The International Community and the Poorest Economies," Michigan State University, Center for Global Development, unpublished paper, February 1, 2004, pp. 3–6.

11. Prahalad, *The Fortune at the Bottom of the Pyramid*.

12. The charter of the World Bank stipulates that its mission is *economic* development and that it is to be strictly *nonpolitical*.

13. See George C. Lodge, *Engines of Change: United States Interests and Revolution in Latin America*, with an introduction by Samuel P. Huntington (New York: Alfred A. Knopf, 1969), chapters 5 and 6.

14. "Enterprise Solutions to Poverty: Opportunities and Challenges for the International Development Community and Big Business," The Shell Foundation, March 2005, pp. 13, 26.

15. *Financial Times*, June 24, 2004, p. 2.

16. Ibid.

17. Clayton Christensen, *The Innovator's Dilemma* (Boston, MA: Harvard Business School Press, 1997); Gary Hamel, *Leading the Revolution* (Boston, MA: Harvard Business School Press, 2000).

18. Rachel Jupp, *Getting Down to Business* (London: Demos, 2002); Giles Gibbons and Steven Hilton, *Good Business, Your World Needs You* (New York: Texere, 2002).

19. *Financial Times*, June 24, 2004, p. 2.

## Chapter 7
### The Options for Business Contributions

1. Milton Friedman, *Capitalism and Freedom*, p. 133.

2. Ian Davis, "The Biggest Contract," *The Economist*, May 26, 2005, pp. 73, 75.

3. Numerous developing countries, and operators within them, are keen to embrace change. For example, numerous developing-country bankers are studying sustainable lending practices. Bangladesh is a case in point. The bankers, individually at least, are quick to understand the reasons behind the push toward sustainable lending, but they are equally aware of the difficulties of implementing these lending principles in practice. Nobody wants to go first, and alone. The IFC is delivering Sustainable Financial Management training

to bankers worldwide. Many of the principles are much the same as the Equator Principles adopted by some of the world's larger banks.

4. P. Drucker, "Will the Corporation Survive?" in "A Survey of the Near Future," *The Economist*, November 3, 2001, p. 16.

5. Holliday et al., *Walking the Talk*, p. 193.

6. Holly J. Gregory, "The Globalisation of Corporate Governance," *Global Counsel*, September and October 2000, p. 2.

7. IBM, 2002 Corporate Social Responsibility Report, CEO Letter.

8. Holliday et al., *Walking the Talk*, p. 109.

9. See Prahalad, *The Fortune at the Bottom of the Pyramid*, and the December 2004 conference convened in San Francisco, California, by the World Resources Institute, "Eradicating Poverty Through Profit."

10. Narayan et al., *Voices of the Poor*.

11. Peter Woicke, prepared remarks to the SRI in the Rockies Conference, Keystone, Colorado, October 8, 2004, p. 3.


*Chapter 8*
*A World Development Corporation*


1. In each of these countries, except Japan, foreign direct investment by the world's MNCs played a central role. In Vietnam, for example, in 2003 FDI was worth more than 8 percent of the GDP, and poverty had declined from 58 percent of the population in 1993 to 29 percent in 2002 (*The Economist*, May 8, 2004, p. 39).

2. May 22, 2004, p. 20.

3. William W. Lewis, "The Power of Productivity," *McKinsey Quarterly* 2 (2004): 101ff.

# Bibliography

Annan, Kofi A. *We the Peoples: The Role of the United Nations in the 21st Century.* New York: United Nations, 2000.

Annan, Kofi. Speech to the World Economic Forum, February 2002, quoted in Judy Shelton, "More Aid? Sounds Great but Wait . . . ," *Wall Street Journal*, February 15, 2002, p. A16.

"A Survey of America." *The Economist*, November 8, 2003, p. 19.

Austin, James. *The Collaboration Challenge: How Non-Profits and Business Succeed Through Strategic Alliances.* San Francisco: Jossey-Bass, 2000.

Bendell, Jim, and David F. Murphy. *Partners in Time? Business, NGOs and Sustainable Development.* Geneva: UNRISD, 1999.

Berle, Adolf A., and Gardiner C. Means. *The Modern Corporation and Private Property.* New York: Harcourt, Brace & World, 1967.

Berman, Jonathan E., and Tobias Webb. "Race to the Top: Attracting and Enabling Global Sustainable Business—Business Survey Report." Washington, D.C.: World Bank Group, Corporate Social Responsibility Practice, October 2003.

Blackett, Adelle. Symposium: "Globalization, Accountability, and the Future of Administrative Law: Global Governance, Legal Pluralism and the Decentered State: A Labor Law Critique of Codes of Corporate Conduct." *Indiana Journal of Global Legal Studies* (Spring 2001).

Bradford, Colin, and Johannes F. Linn. "Global Economic Governance at a Crossroads: Replacing the G-7 with the G-20." Washington, D.C.: Brookings Institution, April 2004.

Brainard, Lael, et al. *The Other War: Global Poverty and the Millennium Challenge Account.* Washington, D.C.: Center for Global Development and Brookings Institution Press, 2003.

Braithwaite, John, and Peter Drahos. *Global Business Regulation.* Cambridge: Cambridge University Press, 2000.

Chandler, Alfred D. Jr. *The Visible Hand: The Managerial Revolution in American Business.* Cambridge, MA: Harvard University Press, 1977.

Chandler, Alfred, and Bruce Mazlish, eds. *Leviathans: Multinational Corporations and the New Global History.* Cambridge: Cambridge University Press, 2005.

Christensen, Clayton. *The Innovator's Dilemma.* Boston, MA: Harvard Business School Press, 1997.

Commission on Private Sector Development to the Secretary-General of the United Nations. "Unleashing Entrepreneurship: Making Business Work for the Poor." New York: United Nations Development Program, 2004.

Davis, Ian. "The Biggest Contract." *The Economist,* May 26, 2005, pp. 73, 75.

Destutt de Tracy, Antoine L. *Elemens d'Ideologie,* 2nd ed. Brussels: A. Wahlen, 1826.

Dicey, Albert V. *Lectures on the Relation Between Law and Public Opinion in England During the Nineteenth Century.* London: Macmillan, 1952.

Drucker, Peter. "Will the Corporation Survive?" In "The Next Society: A Survey of the Near Future." *The Economist,* November 3, 2001, p. 16.

Edwards, Michael. *Civil Society.* Cambridge, UK: Polity Press, 2004.

Elliott, Kimberly Ann, and Richard B. Freeman. "White Hats or Don Quixote? Human Rights Vigilantes in the Global Economy," National Bureau of Economics Research Working Paper No. 8102, 2001, Cambridge, MA.

"Eradicating Poverty Through Profit." Conference in San Francisco, CA. West Palm Beach, FL: World Resources Institute, December 2004.

European Union. 2003 European Conference on Corporate Social Responsibility: The Role of Public Policies in Promoting CSR, conference booklet.

Fidler, Stephen. "Who's Minding the Bank?" *Foreign Policy* 126 (September/October 2001): 40–50.

Friedman, Milton. *Capitalism and Freedom.* Chicago: University of Chicago Press, 1982.

Gabel, Medard, and Henry Bruner. *Globalinc: An Atlas of the Multinational Corporation.* New York: New Press, 2003.

Gereffi, Gary, Ronie Garcia-Johnson, and Erika Sasser. "The NGO-Industrial Complex." *Foreign Policy* 125 (July/August 2001): 56–65.

Ghandi, Sanjay, and Bouri Sandhouidi. "Madagascar Launches Pro-Poor Initiative by Business." New York: UNDP Press Release, January 5, 2004.

Gibbons, Giles, and Steve Hilton. *Good Business, Your World Needs You.* New York: Texere, 2002.

Goodwin, Neva R. "The Social Impact of Multinational Corporations: An Outline of Issues with a Focus on Workers." In Alfred Chandler and Bruce Mazlish, eds., *Leviathans: Multinational Corporations and the New Global History.* Cambridge: Cambridge University Press, 2005.

Greenhouse, Linda. "Human Rights Abuses Worldwide Are Held to Fall under U.S. Courts." *New York Times,* June 30, 2004, p. A21.

Gregory, Holly J. "The Globalisation of Corporate Governance." *Global Counsel,* September and October 2000.

Gunter, Bernhard G., and Rolph van der Hoeven. "The Social Dimension of Globalization: A Review of the Literature." *International Labor Review* 143 (Geneva: International Labour Organization, 2004), pp. 7–19.

Hamel, Gary. *Leading the Revolution*. Boston, MA: Harvard Business School Press, 2000.

Henderson, David. *Misguided Virtue: False Notions of Corporate Social Responsibility*. London: Institute of Economic Affairs, 2001.

Hodgson, Geoffrey M. *How Economics Forgot History: The Problem of Historical Specificity in Social Science*. London and New York: Routledge, 2001.

Hoffman, Kurt. "Enterprise Solutions to Poverty: Opportunities and Challenges for the International Development Community and Big Business." The Shell Foundation, March 2005, pp. 13, 26.

Holliday, Charles O., Stephan Schmidheiny, and Philip Watts. *Walking the Talk: The Business Case for Sustainable Development*. Sheffield, UK: Greenleaf Publishing, 2002.

Huntington, Samuel. *American Politics: The Promise of Disharmony*. Cambridge, MA: Harvard University Press, 1981.

IBM. 2002 Corporate Social Responsibility Report.

International Business Leaders Forum and World Business Council for Sustainable Development. A Business Guide to Development Actors, IBLF/WBCSD, 2004.

International Chamber of Commerce. Press Releases: "ICC Calls for Swift Conclusion of Doha Round." Washington, D.C., June 9, 2004.

International Finance Corporation. *Measuring Sustainability: A Framework for Private Sector Investments*. Washington, D.C., 2003.

International Finance Corporation. *Sustainable Investment*. Washington, D.C., 2004.

Jorgensen, Helle B., Peder M. Pruzan-Jorgensen, Margaret Jungk, and Aron Cramer. "Strengthening Implementation of Corporate Social Responsibility in Global Supply Chains." Washington, D.C.: World Bank Group, Corporate Social Responsibility Practice, October 2003.

Jupp, Rachel. *Getting Down to Business*. London: Demos, 2002.

Klein, Michael, and Tim Hartford. "Corporate Responsibility: When Will Voluntary Reputation Building Improve Standards?" In *Public Policy for the Private Sector*, Note Number 271. Washington, D.C.: International Finance Corporation, May 1, 2004.

Korbin, Stephen J. "Multinational Corporations, the Protest Movement, and the Future of Global Governance." In Alfred Chandler and Bruce Mazlish, eds., *Leviathans: Multinational Corporations and the New Global History*. Cambridge: Cambridge University Press, 2005.

Kuhn, Thomas S. *The Structure of Scientific Revolutions*. Chicago and London: University of Chicago Press, 1962.

"Leaders: No Democracy Please, We're Shareholders." *The Economist*, May 1, 2004, p. 13.

"Les Etats-Unis Informant la Conference du Disarmament du Plan d'Action du G-8 en Matiere de non-Proliferation." New York: UN Press Release, June 10, 2004.

Lewis, William W. "The Power of Productivity." *McKinsey Quarterly* 2 (2004): 101.

"Linking International Trade with Poverty Reduction." *The Least Developed Countries Report 2004*. Geneva: UNCTAD, 2004.

Litvin, Daniel. "Memorandum to Kofi Annan." *Foreign Policy* 139 (November–December 2003): 68.

"Living With the Enemy—How Firms Should Treat Non-Governmental Organizations." *The Economist*, August 9, 2003, p. 55.

Lodge, George C. *Engines of Change: United States Interests and Revolution in Latin America*. New York: Alfred A. Knopf, 1969.

Lodge, George C. "Business and the Changing Society." *Harvard Business Review* 52 (March–April 1974): 59–72.

Lodge, George C. *The New American Ideology*. New York: Alfred A. Knopf, 1975.

Lodge, George C. *Managing Globalization in the Age of Interdependence*. Johannesburg and San Diego: Pfeiffer, 1995.

Lodge, George C. "The Corporate Key: Using Big Business to Fight Global Poverty." *Foreign Affairs* 82 (July–August 2002): 13.

Lodge, George C. *The Legitimacy of Business*. Conference paper, Philosophy of Management Conference, St. Anne's College, Oxford, July 2004.

Lodge, George C., and Ezra F. Vogel, eds. *Ideology and National Competitiveness: An Analysis of Nine Countries*. Boston, MA: Harvard Business School Press, 1987.

Luetkenhorst, Wilfried. "UNIDO Partnership Programme: Joining Hands with Business to Promote Industrial Development." Vienna: UNIDO, 2000.

Mannheim, Karl. *Ideogy and Utopia*. New York: Harcourt Brace, 1953.

McCraw, Thomas K. "The Trouble with Adam Smith." *American Scholar* 61 (1992): 371.

McKinsey Global Institute. *New Horizons: Multinational Company Investment in Developing Countries*. Washington, D.C., October 2003.

"Measuring Globalization." *Foreign Policy* 141 (March/April 2004): 54–69.

Narayan, Deepa, et al. "Voices of the Poor." Washington, D.C., and Oxford: World Bank, Oxford University Press, 2000.

Neal, Christopher, and Cynthia Case. "Global Poverty Down by Half Since 1981." World Bank News Release No: 2004/309/S. Washington, D.C., April 23, 2004.

Nelson, Jane, and Dave Prescott. "Business and the Millennium Development Goals: A Framework for Action." London: International Business Leaders Forum, 2003.

Novak, Michael. *The Catholic Ethic and the Spirit of Capitalism.* New York: Free Press, 1993.

OECD. "Foreign Direct Investment for Development: Maximising Benefits, Minimising Costs." Paris: OECD, 2002.

*Oxford English Dictionary,* 2nd edition. Oxford: Oxford University Press, 1989.

Pitcher, George. "Corporate Responsibility Doesn't Cost the Earth." *Marketing Week,* September 12, 2002, p. 25.

Political and Economic Consulting. *Race to the Top: Attracting and Enabling Global Sustainable Business—Business Survey Report.* World Bank Group, 2003.

Prahalad, C. K. *The Fortune at the Bottom of the Pyramid: Eradicating Poverty Through Profits.* Upper Saddle River, NJ: Wharton School Publishing, 2004.

"Preliminary Report on the Global Compact Leaders Summit." New York: UN Global Compact Office, July 2, 2004.

Roach, Brian. "A Primer on Multinational Corporations." In Alfred Chandler and Bruce Mazlish, eds., *Leviathans: Multinational Corporations and the New Global History.* Cambridge: Cambridge University Press, 2005.

Ruggie, John G. "Taking Embedded Liberalism Global." In David Held and Mathias Koenig-Archibugi, *Taming Globalization: Frontiers of Governance.* Cambridge, UK: Polity Press, 2003.

Sachs, Jeffrey D. "Globalization and Patterns of Economic Growth." In Michael M. Weinstein, ed., *Globalization: What's New.* New York: Columbia University Press, 2005, p. 214.

Simmons, P. J. "Learning to Live with NGOs." *Foreign Policy* 112 (Fall 1998): 82–96.

Simmons, P. J., and Chantal de Jonge Oudrant, eds. *Managing Global Issues: Lessons Learned.* Washington, D.C.: Carnegie Endowment for International Peace, 2001.

Stiglitz, Joseph E. *Globalization and Its Discontents.* New York: Norton, 2002.

"Strengthening Grassroots Business Organization Initiative." Washington, D.C.: International Finance Corporation, 2004.

SustainAbility and UN Global Compact. "Gearing Up: From Corporate Responsibility to Good Governance and Scalable Solutions." London: SustainAbility, January 2004.

Teilhard de Chardin, Pierre. *The Future of Man*, translated by Norman Denny. New York: Harper and Row, 1964.

"The Good Pupil; Vietnam's Economy." *The Economist*, May 8, 2004, p. 63.

Thiessen, Marc A. "When Worlds Collide." *Foreign Policy* 123 (March/April 2001): 64–74.

UN Conference on Trade and Development. *Development and Globalization: Facts and Figures*. New York: United Nations, 2004.

UN Conference on Trade and Development and Sustainable Business Institute, European Business School. "Making FDI Work for Sustainable Development." New York: United Nations, 2004.

UNDP. "Report on the Launch of the Growing Sustainable Business Initiative in Tanzania." New York: United Nations, September 2003.

UNDP, Commission on the Private Sector and Development. "Unleashing Entrepreneurship: Making Business Work for the Poor." New York: United Nations, 2004.

UNDP and International Business Leaders Forum. "Business and the Millennium Development Goals." New York: United Nations, 2003.

UNDP, UN International Development Organization, and UN Global Compact. "Partnerships for Small Enterprise Development." New York: United Nations, January 2004.

UN Global Compact and the UNDP. "Growing Sustainable Business for Poverty Reduction." New York: United Nations, 2004.

UN Global Compact Office. "Preliminary Report on the Global Compact Leaders Summit." New York: United Nations, July 2, 2004.

UNIDO. *Operationalizing UNIDO's Corporate Strategy: Services and Priorities for the Medium Term, 2004–2007*. Vienna: UN International Development Office, 2003.

UNIDO, Corporate Social Responsibility. "Implications for Small and Medium Enterprises in Developing Countries." New York: UN International Development Office, 2002.

Vernon, Raymond. *Sovereignty at Bay: The Multinational Spread of U.S. Enterprise*. New York: Basic Books, 1971.

Vernon, Raymond. "Rogue Elephant in the Forest: An Appraisal of Transatlantic Relations." *Foreign Affairs* 51 (April 1973): 573–587.

Waldman, Peter. "Washington's Tilt to Business Stirs a Backlash in Indonesia." *Wall Street Journal*, February 11, 2004, p. 1.

Walter, Andrew. "NGOs, Business and International Investment: the Multi-lateral Agreement on Investment, Seattle, and Beyond." *Global Governance* 7 (January–March, 2001): 51.

World Bank. "Timor-Leste—Poverty in a New Nation: Analysis for Action." Washington, D.C.: World Bank, May 2003.

World Bank. "Global Monitoring Report 2004: Policies and Actions for Achieving the Millennium Development Goals and Related Outcomes." Washington, D.C.: World Bank, 2004.

World Bank. "Poverty Reduction Strategy Paper Sourcebook." Washington, D.C.: World Bank Group, March 11, 2004.

World Bank. *World Development Indicators 2004*. Washington, D.C.: World Bank, 2004.

# Index